How to succeed in
Newspaper
Journalism

David Stephenson

**KOGAN
PAGE**

The masculine pronoun is used throughout this book. This is for ease and clarity only and no prejudice or bias is intended

YOURS TO HAVE AND TO HOLD
BUT NOT TO COPY

First published in 1998

Kogan Page Limited
120 Pentonville Road
London N1 9JN

© David Stephenson 1998

British Library Cataloguing in Publication Data

A CIP record for this book is avaible from the British Library

ISBN 0 7494 2514 8

Typeset by Kogan Page
Printed and bound in Great Britian by Clays Ltd, St Ives plc

Contents

Preface   *ix*

1   What is journalism?   **1**
How to succeed in newspapers *1*
Are you a typical journalist? *4*
The life cycle of a newspaper story *4*

2   What is news?   **8**
Old news is bad news *11*
Nothing but the truth *12*

3   News reporting   **14**
The working life of a reporter *15*
Contacts *16*
Getting to know contacts *18*
Covering a general news story *19*
Handouts and agency copy *22*
Interviewing *24*
Press conferences *27*
Speeches *31*
The vox pop *34*
Doorstops, all-ins and death knocks *36*

4   News writing   **38**
Creating a news story *38*
The structure of a news story *39*
Choosing an angle *46*
Writing the intro *47*
Who, what, where, when, why and how? *48*
Structuring your story *53*
Story checklist *58*

Running stories and breaking news *59*

5   General features   **61**
Why features? *61*
How do we define a feature? *63*
Types of features *65*
How to find your style *69*
Style to suit *71*
The structure of features *72*
Writing feature intros *75*

6   Specialist features   **80**
Profiles *80*
Profile types *82*
How to structure a profile *83*
The cuttings job *86*
Face-to-face interviews *87*
Embarrassing questions *89*
Colour *90*
Writing the story *92*
Reviews *94*
Writing a review *95*
Libel *96*
Leader articles *98*
How to write a leader *101*
Personal columns *102*

7   Other forms of journalism   **107**
Production journalism *107*
The role of the sub *107*
Photojournalism *111*

8   Getting started   **115**
Roles in newspaper journalism *115*
Training to be a journalist *118*

Glossary   *131*

Answers   *135*

Further reading 139

Index 141

Preface

The idea for this book came after teaching courses on news and feature writing to MA journalism postgraduate students at the
University of Westminster. I felt there was a need for a book that
was written by a working newspaper journalist. While much of what
I have written is based on these courses in newspaper journalism,
this book is aimed at all media studies students: at GCSE level, A-
level and undergraduate. But if you wish to pursue a career in radio
or TV journalism, this is not the book for you. It deals specifically
with what makes a newspaper story, how to report one, how to
write it and newspaper features. Throughout the book, there are also
exercises that you can use to improve your practical journalism
skills. The answers can be found on pages 135 to 138. There is also
a comprehensive chapter on training, which details how to get a
training place on a newspaper, along with a full list of colleges and
courses accredited by the National Council for the Training of
Journalists.

1

What is journalism?

When we think of journalism, we think of someone writing for a newspaper or magazine. This is still largely the case but journalism is changing all the time. Technology has meant that journalists and reporters now work on radio, television, news agencies and other electronic on-line services.

There is no doubt that the demand for information has changed the way we think about journalism. The benefit of this revolution is that there are more opportunities for journalists and they are more varied. Already people who specialize in radio and television are 'bi-medial', but soon journalists will need to be 'multi-medial', spreading their talents across different fields. This means that the journalistic skills you learn at this stage of your career need to be relevant to any form of media. When you do come to move jobs, all you will need to do is retrain on new technology.

So much for the different forms of media but what of the 'stuff' of journalism, what is actually written? While it is true that news and current events still constitute the bulk of what is written in papers and magazines, there is now a trend towards what could be called 'information journalism', which is written in a way that is both interesting and accessible.

How to succeed in newspapers

Clearly a journalist must be multi-talented, but what are the essential qualities that you need to succeed in this field? To climb to the top of the journalistic tree, you will need determination, dedication, stamina, good general knowledge, intelligence, inquisitiveness,

what i learnt I need

resourcefulness, imagination, confidence and a sense of humour. You will also need a double measure of good luck which, in most cases, falls back on 'being in the right place, at the right time'. But given the pace with which some magazines and newspapers close, reopen and relaunch, the 'right time' has a habit of coming round a little more frequently nowadays.

Determination is perhaps the most important quality. Given the competitive nature of journalism and the limited number of inter-esting positions on papers and magazines, you will need to remain focused on your goals to achieve them. If it is your ambition to become a feature writer on a national daily newspaper you will face the stiffest of competition from other journalists who are equally single-minded to satisfy their ambitions. Should you suffer a small setback, you will need to view this philosophically before becoming doubly determined. If your first job is on a local newspaper, the thought of reaching a national journal may seem a distant one. But the reality is that this is one of the best training grounds possible and such a paper can be merely the first step on the ladder.

You must also be dedicated. This means that you need to be aware of the responsibilities of a journalist. For dedication, you can also read integrity – a quality that you will need in order to inspire confidence in those around you, especially those upon which you will rely for information and stories.

Intelligence is a key quality. Your ability to assess information or a situation quickly will separate you immediately from those who can-not. The reason is that all journalism is about speed – the time that it takes you to put together a story, write 500 words on a subject or track down someone who will speak informatively about a particu-lar issue. Deadlines are ever present and a high level of intelligence will mean that you will reach the right conclusion before anyone else. Intelligence does not mean intellect. It is not your role to deliv-er the most abstruse interpretation of a certain event; no one will be interested and it will serve only to boost your ego. The readers are paramount in all these judgements and you must always consider their needs first.

Inquisitiveness is another essential quality. It is the ability to be able to look at a set of facts that may appear very ordinary to one person but to you throw up a whole series of unanswered ques-tions. It will be your job to pursue these questions until you are satisfied with the answers Fundamentally it means you ask 'who, what, when, where, why and how' each time you come across a potential story.

Resourcefulness is another important factor. Essentially, journalism is a job for individualistic people, and your level of self-reliance will be critical. On the first day of your first job as a reporter on a local paper you may be asked to find three drug addicts to expose the local drug problems. Immediately, you will need to source these people by whichever means you can. There are numerous other situations in which you will need to think on your feet and being streetwise will help.

Imagination is a very necessary quality because much of the news you chase can be very tedious. This is not to say that the chase itself is not interesting, but thinking of new ways to write and research the same subject requires creativity. If you are a crime correspondent, for instance, you will cover many murders but the difference between your report and someone else's will be your determination to find a new 'angle' or a new way of looking at a story.

Confidence is a quality that may not happen immediately but it is one that has a tendency to drive all the other character traits that I have mentioned. The more you do in journalism, the better you will become and in turn your confidence will increase. This will improve your judgement and help you to trust your instincts or a hunch over particular stories. The more confident you become, the more people will trust your judgement.

A good sense of humour in journalism is highly rated by editors. Always try to see the lighter side of events, obviously not where tragedy is involved, but where life itself seems ridiculous or absurd. It will improve your writing and encourage you not to see life as a serious journey from one story to the next. A light touch to your work can also help a reader's understanding of a subject and can be very entertaining. You will also need stamina, as journalists often have to work very long hours.

Finally, to succeed as a journalist you should have a strong sense of ethics. A good lead is provided by the journalists' body, the National Union of Journalists, which has a Code of Conduct that sets down the responsibilities of a practising journalist. These include maintaining the highest ethical standards, reporting in a fair and accurate way, eliminating inaccuracies, protecting your own sources and not accepting bribes or inducements. Another source on conduct is the Press Complaints Commission (PCC), which publishes its own Code of Practice for working journalists.

So does one need to be born with all the above qualities to succeed in journalism? In short, no. Each one can be developed over time and some will enhance others as you become more experienced. How do you acquire them? Much of this will depend on your level of education and training (see Chapter 8).

Are you a typical journalist?

You may feel you have the necessary qualities to be a journalist, but do you recognize yourself in this survey? The London College of Printing carried out a poll of 726 journalists (about 5 per cent of the total) and found that the 'modern British journalist is white, mainstream, middle-class and verging on the middle age'. He drinks carefully and hardly ever smokes. Half of those polled did not have children but the other half would recommend journalism as a career to their children. The median age is 38. Some other findings were:

- 57 per cent vote Labour
- 6 per cent vote Conservative
- 20 per cent earned over £35,000, while 32 per cent earned between £15,000 and £25,000
- 50 per cent want to keep the Royal Family
- 75 per cent are in favour of legalizing prostitution
- 96 per cent are in favour of condom vending machines.

The life cycle of a newspaper story

A news or feature story begins life as an idea. This can originate from many sources: staff reporters, news or features editor, the paper's editor, freelance writer, indeed anyone on the editorial staff. The idea will generally end up with the features or news editor who will decide whether it merits a story and, if it has been written already, whether it can go forward to production in its present form.

If the idea has come from a news reporter, the news editor will take it forward to a morning conference and include it on a list of 'possibles' for the first edition. Should it be a strong contender for the edition, a reporter will be assigned before the conference.

When an idea has originated from a freelance writer, the features editor, for instance, will again submit it to the conference but not usually give any go-ahead to the writer until the editor has approved the idea. If a story idea comes out of conference, the news and features editor will discuss who should write the piece before it is commissioned.

Once the idea has been approved, we reach the next stage: the writing. There is surprisingly little time to write a story on a newspaper if it is to go into the first edition. Ideally, all news and features copy should be sent to the news or features editor by four o'clock in the afternoon, if you are working for a morning paper, so that it can be read and any possible changes and rewrites done. Evening paper journalists have to deliver their copy usually before eight o'clock in the morning and, frequently, the night before. On a weekly magazine, you may have to file your copy up to three weeks before the actual publication date to allow for colour processing and printing. If you are to write a feature for a morning paper, you may discover that it is for the following day as features departments tend to work in advance, putting together a weekly section as and when the stories become available.

If it is a news story, it will be sent to the news editor by the early evening. The editor will read it through to make sure it is exactly what had been expected and then pass it through to the chief sub-editor for subbing and production. In the meantime, the news editor will have discussed with the 'chief sub' how they imagine the story will look on the final printed page. They will then choose a 'shape' or 'scheme' for the story, in conjunction with the other items that will appear on that page. The shape is actually how long the story will run (300 or 400 words, for instance) and over how many columns of the page. This will depend on whether a picture is to be used and the importance of the story. The picture editor or a researcher will then be asked if a suitable photograph of the subject can be found. This may be something from stock or perhaps a 'snapper' (photographer) has been sent out to take a few pictures of the event.

At any of the these stages, of course, the story may 'fall down' completely. Often, with a news piece, the story can change in some way that makes it less of a story and thus not worth running. Another reason is that other stories may have become more important and push your story from page 2 to page 10, for instance. If a story had been 'planned' for a page, it is likely that another home for it would be found. This is where competition begins for a journalist: not only are you competing with reporters from other newspapers who might get the story, there are also the other stories from colleagues that will be competing for your space. It is essential at this point that you deliver good copy to your editor.

Your story has now passed the editorial hurdle – for the time being – and has been handed over to the production department for subbing. The chief sub-editor will now farm out your copy to a 'down table' or junior sub-editor who will read the story, looking for any factual oversights or grammatical departures, but who will mostly ensure that it makes sense. This is the first of a series of fresh eyes who will look at your story as if for the first time, much as if they were a reader. At this point you may well be called upon to make certain changes or rewrite sections.

If it receives a warm welcome from a sub-editor, it will be passed back to chief sub having been 'set' or put on the page in the space that you eventually see it in the newspaper. It will have a headline, any captions and, it is hoped, will be free from any spelling errors. There is little to stop the story going to press now, save a calamity that engulfs that first five pages, or the lawyer. If you work on a national paper, the duty solicitor or barrister will read through your copy, making sure that you have not libelled anyone. If hee does have concerns, you may be asked to clarify certain points and change the copy in places. In most circumstances, lawyers have the power of veto of a story and can kill it if they feel it will cost the company money. Also, all qualified journalists should be versed in libel and contempt law.

When the page in which the story appears has been completely subbed it will then go back to the editor of your department (news, sport, features, city) for a final read and approval. It is likely that the editor may also read over the page at this point, depending on the importance of the story. Once the head of department has given the all-clear, the production editor will 'send' the page to what is known as the print site, where the presses (hence the term, the Press) will start rolling. The next time the story appears is in the newspaper the following morning.

2

What is news?

This is one of the most difficult questions for a student journalist to grasp. But you can take consolation from the fact that it has also taxed many media theorists who seem no closer to coming up with a satisfactory definition. Even most working journalists will give you a strange look if you ask them why they think one story is newsworthy while another is not. They will probably tell you that it is an instinctive decision on their part.

Here are a few quotes to help you think about the meaning of news. The first is from the American journalist John Bogart: 'When a dog bites a man, that is not news, because it happens so often. But if a man bites a dog, that is news.' This illustrates the importance of the 'newness' of news, where the incidence of a man biting a dog is significantly less than of a dog biting a man. It is therefore worth a story.

The second is: 'News is something someone somewhere doesn't want you to know.' While apparently a nonsense at first glance, this quote highlights the investigative nature of news. It says that a story is only news if it is being concealed by someone and any information that is freely available to a journalist will not be worth knowing, and therefore not particularly interesting to the reader.

Here is another: 'News is something interesting that I didn't know yesterday.' And finally, English novelist (and former journalist) Evelyn Waugh from *Scoop*: 'News is what a chap who doesn't care much about anything wants to read. And it's only news until he's read it. After that it's dead.'

While there is no broad agreement on 'what is news?', it is possible to outline a few common characteristics. The first thing we can say is that news needs to have an aspect of human interest. Some argue that there is too much emphasis on human interest stories in journalism. They say stories should revolve around ideas. This seems to ignore the fact that ideas will eventually affect people in some way, and therefore become human interest stories in the end.

Two factors influence the magnitude of the story: the person involved and the event or occurrence itself. Take the example of President Clinton, one of the most photographed people in the world. Let us say he is involved in a slight traffic accident in Washington while travelling in his chauffeur-driven car.

In a nearby street on the same morning, there is an accident involving a lorry and a car in which a young man is killed. In the accident involving the President no one is injured and there are no suspicious circumstances, but we have a picture of Bill joking with a passer-by after the accident. Which story, do you think, makes the front page? Sadly, the lorry accident is unlikely to make the front page, but both stories might well be linked since they occurred in the same area on the same morning. It is unlikely however that the lorry accident will receive more coverage than the President's mishap, even though someone was killed.

This example shows that, in general terms, the 'person' has now become more important than the 'event'. One reason is the cult of celebrity that now dominates our news agenda and at times highlights our apparently perverse news values. This cult covers members of the Royal Family, 'soap' stars, national beer-swilling champions, pigeon racers, even the odd politician. The result is that many 'events' covered in the newspaper are often trivial in nature because celebrity status is more important. Journalists will often talk about someone as being 'newsworthy'. This simply says that a person is a 'newsmaker', by virtue of who they are or what they do.

The late Diana, Princess of Wales, was the closest that one person has ever come to being considered a 'story' in herself. In normal circumstances stories 'happen' to people. However, with Princess Diana, *she* became the 'story' and events, however trivial, would be reported, sometimes with little thought as to whether they were news.

In many cases, the newsmaker has an important job or role that can alter the way that we lead our lives. Politicians fall immediately into this category: they are newsmakers of the highest order and some would say that they go out of their way to be so. The Home

Secretary, for example, has a responsibility over a huge range of public affairs, not least law and order, which will eventually interest us all. So when he makes an announcement regarding crime, for instance, it is likely that this will be a newsworthy event. Here, the announcement itself is more important than the person making it.

We have now come across another important characteristic of news – it must affect people. If it touches upon people's lives in any significant way, it can generally be said to be a newsworthy happening. This does not mean that as a journalist you need to count the number of people involved in any one story, but often a quick calculation will help you understand the importance of a particular event. One newsworthy event that can absorb practically everyone in the country is the weather. It is surprising just how often the weather makes the news in its various forms, from floods to drought, heat waves to cold spells. They all touch us in various ways and it is a safe bet that most people will be talking about it, too. Other natural occurrences, such as earthquakes or meteor strikes, also fall into this category though thankfully we have few of the latter.

everyone has an interest in the weather.

This leads us to another essential aspect of news – drama. As news invariably involves people and events, the most dramatic combination of the two is often highly newsworthy. Drama can be found elsewhere. One arena, which is a popular source of news, is the law court. Two examples are the O J Simpson case and the Louise Woodward trial in the United States. Here, the court is a theatre of real-life human drama that is reported daily, from theft to murder. The court correspondent simply has to sit and take notes and a story will eventually drop into his lap (often the challenge for a junior reporter is to cover three court cases at once in some larger court buildings). Obviously many people are murdered and many thefts take place, so what is the aspect, other than drama, that determines whether a court appearance will make the news? The answer is the 'interest' factor and a third characteristic of news.

The interest factor is by far the most subjective of all considerations. This is where the individual journalist must ask: is this story interesting? If you cannot satisfy yourself that what you have seen or heard is interesting, it is unlikely that anyone else will. It is your turn to play editor in a sense, to choose what you think will be found interesting by your readers and ignore what isn't. It is more likely that you will be sent by your news editor to cover a particular story rather than having to decide between several, but you will still be required to choose one fact over another. Always ask: Is it news? Why is it news? Would my readers find this interesting?

Old news is bad news

One factor that will almost certainly determine if something is news is whether that 'something' can be said to be new. In fact, it is only in features (see Chapters 5 and 6) where 'newness' can be almost ignored if other criteria are satisfied. Because of its very nature, news cannot be 'old' as most readers will not be interested in a story that they have already come across. In this respect old news is bad news.

This raises another important aspect of news – what is known as the 'angle' or 'hook'. The person involved in a story may not be 'new', for example President Clinton pops up in newspapers all the time. However, the angle of the story is new: a traffic accident involving his limousine. This is crucial to understanding news.

Do any of the earlier story examples have an angle? The meteor strike seems to be without an angle yet immediately strikes you as a news story. The reason is that some subjects are news in themselves, irrespective of what angle is used. In the case of a meteor strike, the angles would be multiple: casualties, rescue, damage, danger of more strikes. Why? In stories where the news impact is obvious, eg natural disasters, the angle is less important until you come to 'follow it up' the next day.

In the case of an announcement by the Home Secretary, the angle is all important. Statements from the Home Office are almost a daily occurrence and often go off without being reported in the press. This is also true with most crime, but if the Home Secretary is to announce a large fall in reported crime this would then become news. It is a new angle on a subject that will interest and affect people, and indeed draws in most of the important characteristics of a good news story.

Does a news story have to be serious? No. News stories definitely have a lighter side and you will notice from popular tabloid papers that this is the side of news that they like to emphasize. 'Freddie Starr ate my hamster', which appeared in *The Sun*, shouldn't be taken seriously (unless you're the hamster) and certainly has no important consequences for the world economy. Indeed, if you examine most stories in the popular tabloid press you will see that even the most serious ones are written in a humorous way, together with the use of a pun headline or a wacky picture.

However, as you move through the spectrum of newspaper styles, from popular tabloid, to middle market tabloid and then broadsheet, the emphasis on the lighter side of news, so called 'good news', begins to wane. Broadsheets are often called the 'serious press' or the 'heavies' where stories are treated in a more important way. Popular tabloids may choose to cover the same stories but they will be 'packaged' in an entirely different way. This doesn't mean that broadsheets will ignore the lighter side of life. In fact, the term 'basement' refers to the bottom part of the broadsheet newspaper page, where editors often place a story that can lighten the tone of the page.

Nothing but the truth

Does a news story have to be true? Unless it is April Fools' Day, yes. The whole basis of news is that it is recommended to the reader as a true and accurate account of an event or happening. As soon as a story starts to mix fiction with fact, its integrity is lost and so is the interest of the reader. It is important that the reader continues to expect the truth and it is the job of the journalist to ensure that stories do not include opinion, unless they are labelled as opinion pieces.

The Press Complaints Commission has done much to promote a more ethical style of journalism through its Code of Practice. With the continuing possibility of a privacy Bill, the work of the journalist looks likely to be scrutinized even more in the future. Here is the Code of Practice on Accuracy, the first heading in the Code:

> Newspapers and periodicals should take care not to publish inaccurate, misleading or distorted material.

And further on, under the heading of Comment, conjecture and fact:

> Newspapers, while free to be partisan, should distinguish clearly

between comment, conjecture and fact.

The Code, therefore, is quite clear on this point Truth is paramount and if you wish to stray into the realms of opinion, you should look to make a move into features.

The National Union of Journalists also emphasizes the importance of truth in news.

> A journalist shall strive to ensure that the information he/she disseminates is fair and accurate, avoid the expression of comment and conjecture as established fact and falsification by distortion, selection or misrepresentation.

3

News reporting

The job of the news reporter is the front line role in any news organization. As a reporter you are first to uncover the news of the day,
gathering the relevant details and writing up a story. In the next
chapter we shall deal with how to write a news story, but first, let
us look at the news gatherer.

Your role as a reporter is twofold. First, you are required to 'react'
to the news of the day, sometimes providing a fresh lead to an event
or happening. But you should also be 'proactive'. This means initiat-
ing ideas from your own analysis and interpretation of the news of
the day or from your own sources. If you are to become a successful reporter, most of your stories will come from the latter. They will
be what are known as 'scoops', ie no other newspaper is known to
have the story.

Why are 'proactive' stories so important? Most journalism deals
with events that have happened and are already public. Because of
this, other newspapers are likely to be privy to exactly the same
information as your title. Many publications draw their news from
the same sources, the same news and picture agencies, the same
press conferences, the same publicists, even the same public relations companies whose role it is to feed journalists with stories. This
is why when a big news story is covered by every paper, the use of
pictures and facts will not differ greatly. These are the bread-and-butter stories of journalism – reporters write them up daily but they
will not make your editor sit up and listen.

This is why you need to become 'proactive' and unearth something new. If you want to succeed as a reporter, you will need to tell
your editor something that he is not expecting to hear, a story to
grab his interest immediately. Often this may be just a different slant

or angle on a story that has already been covered by the paper. Let us say, for instance, that you have been sent to cover a sentencing in a court, a common assignment for a reporter. After the sentence has been handed down by the judge and you have taken down all the relevant details, you notice in the courtroom a member of the family of the victim, who appears to be quite angry with the judgement.

Outside the court, you speak with this person discreetly and discover that he thinks the sentence has been wholly inadequate. You notice that no other reporter has spoken to your interviewee, who then jumps in a taxi and leaves the court. Welcome to your first scoop. You can tell your editor that here is a story which you believe no other publication will have the following morning. There is the possibility that your interviewee could be tracked down by another newspaper, but other reporters do not seem to have noticed the pained expression on the family member's face in the courtroom.

Once back in the office, you contact the legal team involved to see if an appeal will be made against the 'leniency' of the sentence. You discover that indeed there is going to be an appeal; by this stage you have a good story, which has taken an ordinary sentencing story a step further. You might then contact the Crown Prosecution Service, which brings criminal prosecutions to court on behalf of the police, to obtain their point of view.

Here you can see how keeping alert in the courtroom and spotting a chance reaction on someone's face can lead to an exclusive. Our example may be fiction but this sort of story has happened many times to court correspondents. It is a perfect example of a 'reactive' story, covered by many newspapers, that has become 'proactive' because of the initiative of the reporter. It is always down to you, and you only, to take a story one step further. If you wait for it to fall into your lap, it will have fallen into several other reporters' laps also.

The working life of a reporter

A reporter's life is busy and unpredictable. A reporter rarely arrives for work in the morning with a preconceived notion of how the day will go, unless he was assigned to a story overnight. If you are to achieve a National Vocational Qualification in periodical or regional newspaper journalism, here is a rundown of the type of tasks that you will be called on to carry out. In a sense, this is the reporter's job description.

- Generate story leads ('proactive') by making and maintaining contacts.
- Gather information by arranging activities, carrying out research, covering events, carrying out interviews and identifying and following up other story opportunities.
- Decide on the content of stories and the writing style.
- Write news accurately and to a brief.
- Prepare the copy for transmission to the publication.
- Establish and maintain professional relations with colleagues and with members of the public.
- Deal with contributors, including news agencies and other publications.
- Appreciate the importance of pictures.

In addition you will have a knowledge and understanding of:

- defamation, contempt, copyright, breach of confidence;
- ethical and professional issues, such as independence from advertisers and commercial interests; protecting sources; discrimination on the grounds of race, religious belief or sexual orientation.

Contacts

Contacts are vital for the journalist. Whether you are reporting the proceedings of the local council or the House of Commons, the names you keep in your contacts book will shape the success of everything you write. Why are they so important? The reason that journalists keep a close eye on their contacts books is that most take years to develop. They do not suddenly appear overnight with the home phone numbers of politicians and celebrities; they are accumulated over time, often with great difficulty.

Understandably, many people in the news are reluctant to have their numbers given out – especially to a tabloid journalist. There is also the ethical question of whether it is right to disturb someone on their private home number. On this matter you should take your lead from the Press Complaints Commission (PCC) Code of Conduct, which states that 'intrusions and enquiries into an individual's private life without his or her consent... are not generally acceptable... and can only be justified in the public interest.'

Once you and your editor are satisfied with the validity of your enquiry, the use of a home phone number at a reasonable hour is acceptable, as long as you approach the person politely, apologizing for any inconvenience you may have caused. You will also discover that most people 'in the news' are used to having journalists call them at home.

What sort of people should go in a contacts book? When I started my first reporter's job as a 'stringer' or freelance for a local radio station, I immediately started such a book. Not only did it help me to track down the most relevant interviewee, but it allowed me to do it quickly. If every time you need a phone number, you call directory information, you will soon discover that the competition already has the story.

The best way to start a book is to reach for the telephone directory, making sure it is the most recent that is available. If, for example, you have started a job as a reporter on the local paper, turn to the local borough council listing and make a note of the numbers for the education department, social services, even waste management – you never know when the next strike by refuse collectors will happen. Then make your way through the local emergency services (police, ambulance, fire department) and hospitals (private, too). These numbers will give you the backbone of a contacts book but will not obviously give you the scoops that will lift you from the world of the general reporter.

The next step is to make calls to many of the numbers you have collected from the phone book and tell people who you are and ask who would be the best person to contact if a story breaks. Don't be afraid to ask for out-of-office hours numbers in case stories develop and you need to contact your source. Don't be shy: if you are going to be a good reporter your ability to be able to win people's trust over the telephone will be very important. A good way to gain trust – and elicit a home number from a contact – is to offer your contact numbers to them, saying, 'Don't hesitate to call if you hear of a story for me.' Don't forget: many of the 'contacts' with whom you speak are not obliged to tell you anything, unless of course they are involved in media public relations or a press office and it is their job (even then you may come across reticence). Because of this, it is up to you to use any charm you have to make people feel at ease. Most importantly, don't try to trick people by posing as somebody else. Be straight: it's the best policy (it is also against the PCC Code of Practice to obtain information through misrepresentation, unless it is in the public interest).

There is another reason for making actual contact with these 'potential stories'. It is the hope that in having talked to them and developed some rapport, these people may call you unsolicited one day to say, perhaps in the case of the hospital, that a patient happened to die overnight after being left on a trolley outside ward 13. This may sound unlikely but the truth is that people do contact the media for many reasons and they are more likely to do so if they know a name and have already dealt with the journalist.

In the case of the man who died on the trolley, your contact may in fact be trying to highlight a very serious problem at the hospital. It should be pointed out that it is highly unlikely that any public relations or press office staff would volunteer such information easily. These people tend to follow the line of the management. However, it may be a junior doctor, whom you contacted two months ago over a completely different story but who now wants to expose the inadequacies of the present hospital funding or management. Be cautious, too, about stories offered in this way. Ask yourself if the informant is using you to fulfil another agenda. Even if this is the case you could still have a good story but you should be aware of all sides of an issue.

Getting to know contacts

Establishing good contacts will not take forever, but it will be some time before you can be satisfied with the numbers you have. Copy down every number that you ring, however unimportant it may seem at the time, as this may just be the phone call that means you beat the opposition to a story. One of the more tedious jobs for a journalist is 'making calls' to your contacts to find out 'if there is anything happening'. As a crime reporter, most of my time, not surprisingly, was spent on the phone talking to police, trying to find out if there was a story on their particular patch. And if you are working on a specialist ground, such as crime or business, you will rely on good contacts even more than you do as a general reporter.

Try to develop a relationship with your contacts. Once you have spoken to a contact several times over a period of months, perhaps invite them for a drink or even lunch. This may sound a little too forward or familiar but you will discover that many people open up over a pint. Don't forget that many of your contacts may work in an open plan office where it is difficult to offer confidential information over the telephone. Many workplaces also record employees' telephone conversations, especially in the case of stockbroking houses where the leak of information by an analyst to a business correspondent could be construed as insider dealing. This is an extreme case but most employees will find it difficult to 'gossip' about their field of work over the telephone.

Utilize the expenses that are offered by your employers. In national newspapers and magazines, expenses are offered to journalists who wish to lunch or dine a contact. This may seem odd: why should a journalist be paid to take someone out to lunch? The reason is that it is simply good business to maintain good relations with those who can potentially provide you with a story. Newspapers are careful about costs, so it is in your interests only to lunch or dine those people who are genuine contacts, not your mum and dad!

Covering a general news story

When you begin your career as a news reporter, it is likely that your first assignments will be of a general nature: accidents, press conferences, meetings. When dealing with such stories you should try to cover all the angles that you can. Don't just deal with the immediate story; everybody else will be dealing with that angle. To succeed as a reporter you need to dig a little deeper, as in the earlier court example in which a relative was interviewed.

One type of story that you may be asked to cover as a general reporter is an accident. Let us say you have been sent to the scene of a small rail crash in the South-east on a line that has been newly privatized. The scene of such an accident will probably be chaotic, but try to keep a cool head. It is unlikely that you will be able to get very close to the scene as the emergency services will probably have the area cordoned off. In some cases a special area will be designated for the press, so simply show your press pass, which will be issued by your employer, and you will find yourself with other hacks.

One of the real pitfalls in covering this type of story is that you end up 'following the pack'. It is understandable how this happens. Often there is little information and journalists tend to share any leads that they come across. While this is acceptable to an extent, do not be drawn into sharing everything – they may be your new-found friends but they are also the competition. There is nothing worse than discovering that a colleague at the scene of the same story has scooped you at a rival paper. It is a delicate balance to strike but do not be drawn into sharing every scrap of information you receive.

So, there you are in the compound. What do you do? The first thing to do is to try to get out. Obviously, if it is not permitted do not try, but under all other circumstances see if you can make your own way. See if you can search out a policeman who has been near the damaged carriages. You need to find out the number of casualties, their injuries, who they are. Try to find an ambulance man or paramedic, someone who was the first on the scene. A prime target in these circumstances is an eyewitness, so look beyond the cordoned off area for members of the public. You will often find eyewitnesses still near the scene and keen to talk to members of the press. It is surprising just how co-operative people will be if they know their names will appear in a newspaper. It is your job to exploit this – again, do not be shy.

Another good source at this stage is a member of the train crew. You may spot them being interviewed by police or rail investigators. It is important not to hamper police enquiries so tread carefully. You will often find that a press officer from the rail company or the local police has been assigned to the crash. If this is the case, that person will be issuing statements from any press compound that has been set up. It is here that you will glean the basic information for your story. If it is an accident of some magnitude, a politician may arrive to inspect the scene. Make sure you get some quotes from this person.

You will file your story to the office in a series of 'takes' (several pieces of copy) that will either be transmitted directly through a laptop computer or simply read down the telephone line to a copy-taker who will key the story into the system. Always call the news-room when you have something further to add to the story because they may have picked up leads from their own sources in the office.

Once you have gathered everything you can from the scene of the crash and filed it, you will need to follow up the story in the newsroom. Larger organizations will have other reporters to cover different angles but let us assume that it is your sole responsibility to write the final piece. It is at this stage of covering such a story that you must use your instincts as a journalist by thinking of all the possible angles that might arise. All events, such as this, have conse-quences and it is your job to explore them.

Here is a rail crash where someone has been injured, possibly even died. The immediate question, therefore, is how or why did the accident happen? In many ways your approach to covering a news story is similar to writing it in that you need to assemble certain facts: *who*, *what*, *when*, *where*, *why*, *how*. We will deal with these in greater detail in the next chapter but these 'news questions' are the framework for your final story. They must all be answered factually and without any of your own opinions. Do not forget that a news story is simply an assembly of facts that you have gathered.

So, how do you discover the cause of this accident? You will need to speak with the train-operating company, the police investigators, the transport department, perhaps a local MP, even a local rail enthu-siast who may have a particular knowledge of the line. It will not be easy to uncover any new facts as most accidents become the sub-ject of an immediate enquiry and official spokespeople will not release any information in the meantime. However, keep digging as someone is bound to know something and it is worth establishing good contact with these people at this early stage.

Exercise 1: News sources

Here is part of a column written by the former editor of the *Sunday Express*, Brian Hitchen. List the people you would contact to follow up this story.

Steamed up over power

Technically minded people will scoff and say it is a figment of my imagination. But I'm sure that my kettle is taking longer to boil and that my toaster isn't popping up quite as fast as it used to do. The electric kettle element is not scaled with limestone deposit and there are no loose wires or crumbs in the toaster. But the people at the Electricity Board insist that power hasn't changed, so what can the matter be?

(See page 135 for answers.)

Handouts and agency copy

As a news reporter you will be required to deal with not only the information you gather yourself, but also unsolicited handouts that will arrive on your desk with monotonous regularity. These pieces of information come in an ever increasing variety of forms. It used to be that ordinary letters formed the bulk of communications to journalists, but these now run a long way behind faxes and e-mail.

While technology has helped enormously in the gathering of news, it has also increased the volume of information that a journalist is expected to sift through. Companies selling or publicizing their products will not hesitate to fire off a round of faxes to various news organizations if they feel they have an 'interesting story'. Almost without fail, these 'interesting stories' turn out to be incredibly uninteresting, usually some gimmick aimed at generating publicity. It is your job when receiving such communications to discard everything that might have a whiff of publicity about it. It is not the job of a newspaper to provide free advertising to consumers (plenty of magazines do the job much better), unless, of course, the information deals directly with the availability of a product, such as a Teletubby, in the run-up to Christmas, for example.

You should therefore not feel very guilty in filing most of these faxes in the rubbish bin. It does occasionally happen though that a particular gimmick is newsworthy in itself, in which case you should consider doing a story. One example that caught the public's imagination was the advertising campaign for a certain coffee, where each television ad break was a further chapter in an unfolding love story. Had you received a press release about this, you would have been right to have suggested a story to your editor.

The reality is that this type of originality is rare. The bulk of press releases that you receive will be of a much more mundane nature, from government departments of all descriptions, the police, politicians and PR consultants hired by various companies.

Most of these press releases are penned by press officers employed by their company to give information to the public. While many have had training in news writing, most tend to bury any news story deep within the release. This is because the angle of the story is secondary to promoting the company itself. In the case of a communication from the Government Information Unit, this is the government of the day. While they are not so obviously in the business of selling something, the department will be trying to show itself in a positive light.

In a case involving an electricity company, newspapers were sent a press release informing them that there would be an increase in meter reading. Further down the fax however, the actual story was that the company had been forced to do so because it had carried out an increasing number of inaccurate estimates. You must decide, therefore, which is 'news' and which is 'sell' or 'puff'. It was not an act of deception by the electricity company, but the company was definitely trying to put a 'positive spin' on a negative story, ie it had made a mistake.

When you believe that you have unlocked the real story behind the release (if indeed there is one), you must corroborate each fact. This is not as easy as it sounds because most of the facts will be known only to that particular company so you will need to call other similar companies or an industrywide body or association to verify the information. *Do not accept any information on face value.* In the case of the electricity company, you could contact the regulator, where you could expect to receive an objective response. Do not forget, however, that even the regulator must be seen to be carrying out its job properly and thoroughly, so it is unlikely to say that in the past it has failed to keep a close eye on this particular company. Always look beyond the obvious. *Be suspicious, ever sceptical.*

When you are satisfied that you have all the necessary information write up your story, but not before. If it is agency copy you will need to rewrite it considerably because it won't be written in the style of your newspaper. Agency copy, from a company such as the Press Association or a local wire service, is a good source of information but the facts should always be verified. As a rule, treat agency copy and handouts as a good source of news, not news in itself. It is your job to discover the news behind the release. Get other quotes from your sources to broaden the story – make it more interesting. You should also never take on face value the word of one agency. Always verify the facts because any mistake can be costly, both to your career and possibly to the newspaper.

Interviewing

To gather any news, you must first interview someone. Obviously you could rewrite your handout or piece of agency copy, but this would leave your story without any breadth or integrity. At the heart of every good piece of journalism is the interview, whether it is face-to-face, over the telephone or even by e-mail. There may also be cases where you need to write a list of your questions and post or fax them to your interviewee. This is rare but many celebrities, under the control of agents, like to have the questions vetted beforehand to avoid any potential embarrassment.

Telephone interviewing is the most common form of news gathering and is central to your role as a news reporter. Politeness is the key to a good interview style, though often you may have to push a little harder if your interviewee is evasive or failing to understand the point you are making.

Make it clear to the interviewee at the start of the telephone interview exactly why the quotes are required, ie the nature of the story you are doing. Often you will have to deal with a PR consultant before being able to interview your source. Tell them which publication you're working for, when you expect it to be published, in which section the story will be published and that they will be speaking 'on the record'.

This is a journalistic expression which has lost a lot of value over the years because it has been abused by unethical journalists. 'On the record' means that both parties have an agreement that anything that is said between them can be used as a quote in the final story. If this is not the case, make it plain to the source that it is a strictly 'off the record' chat and that none of it will be used. It is then understood that such a conversation could be used as background to help your understanding of the story but nothing else. This is not to say that some of the 'information' you have gathered during this informal chat cannot become the basis of several paragraphs, but it should not be attributable to the interviewee.

Some interviewees, especially politicians, are in the habit of asking, 'Unattributable? Off the record?' If you answer yes, you have entered into an agreement of trust with your source. If you break this agreement by publishing everything they say, it is likely that this will be the last time you are given an audience. Establish your integrity as a journalist and maintain it under all circumstances because word will quickly spread if you are unscrupulous in your dealings with people. Unattributable, off the record conversations are imperative as often these dialogues are the starting point for a story and, in many instances, begin as an informal chat over the telephone.

So, now you have established the 'status' of the interview. If you do not make it plain to the interviewee that the conversation is off or on the record it is normally assumed that the interview is on the record. There are times when this 'off the record' relationship is abused by the interviewee. This happens when a source wants to reveal something to a journalist but not be 'quoted' in the final story. The best way to avoid this situation is to clarify the position before you start the interview.

If you are recording the conversation, make this known to the source. Again, you are placed in a position of trust: don't abuse it. Most reporters will use a notebook or even key the information directly on to the newspaper computer system to save time. The latter is a little disconcerting for the interviewee, waiting for you to type every response on the keyboard. If possible, key in the quotes from your notebook after the interview. Should the quotes be taken down word for word? The answer is a firm yes. You are making a journalistic record of this conversation and it should be as accurate as possible. Most newspapers will require you to undertake a shorthand course, probably in your own time, but ordinarily this is a skill you should have brought to the job. It cannot be avoided and will make you a better journalist.

The way you conduct the interview itself will have much to do with whether your deadline is pressing. Should you have a few spare minutes beforehand, jot down the odd question, otherwise the process will be relatively off-the-cuff and unstructured. Treat the interview as you would a normal conversation with a friend or colleague and try to keep your questioning as informal as possible. Avoid being pompous or superior or even deigning to know more about the subject than your interviewee does; this will not go down well and your source will become defensive.

If time is at a premium, try to concentrate on getting a good quote on the central point of the story. Let us say that you have got through to the chairman of that electricity company to question him over the handout you have received about metering. First, ask him to confirm what you have read on the release: that the company is going to read more meters. It is likely that the chairman will give you a well rehearsed response to this question, which you will duly take down in your notebook. The next most pertinent question is 'Why?'.

It is your duty as a journalist to keep pressing the chairman, hopefully until he concedes that the increased incidence of meter reading has been caused by inaccuracies in previous estimates. It is not merely that the company feels that it would be a prudent thing to do more meter reading; it is because their billing system seems to be inefficient. Do not give in until you get this response as you will have let the real story pass you by if you do. It is at this point that your instinct as a journalist should come to the fore.

When you sense you have stumbled across a story, pursue it until you get it. In this case, you would like the electricity company chairman to say that he regrets the number of inaccuracies and that he has had to change the system. It is the chairman's job to avoid this eventuality by putting the best possible spin on the story. Your role, through your tenacity, is to push and prod until the right quotes land on your notebook. Of course, all this must take place within the bounds of politeness, but don't be afraid to press your case – many interviewees will expect it. This strategy may sound as though you are being asked to put words into the interviewee's mouth. But really you are asking the interviewee to support your story. It is your instinct, your understanding that 'X' is the truth and getting someone to say 'X' (on the record) that is the real art of reporting.

Press conferences

We will now look at two popular 'set pieces', the first of which is the press conference or 'presser' as it is sometimes known (it is also known as a news conference). Who holds a press conference? The answer is a variety of people, including politicians, police, business people, celebrities – indeed, anyone who believes they have something important to say and would like to tell the media. Fundamentally, it is a way of creating your own 'news event' and inviting the media along to watch. It also saves time. One press conference can replace 20 or more individual interviews.

If you followed the 1997 General Election campaign closely you will have noted how extensively the press conference was used by politicians. All three major parties began each day of campaigning with a 'set piece' press conference at which they attempted to set the agenda for the day's media coverage. At each conference they handed out a press release, in which they detailed their particular theme for the day: health, education, crime, etc. Journalists were then invited to question the minister or shadow minister concerned.

The aim of such a conference is control. Organizations and individuals use the press conference as an attempt to convey their message to the public. By inviting members of the media *en masse*, they can guarantee that the same message is put across to each journalist, even though they have no control over how each reporter will deal with the information. Inevitably, journalists will report and write the story differently, depending on the style and demands of the newspaper or television channel.

Not only do you have no control at a press conference, but you will also not get an exclusive. Since journalists will be invited from most news organizations, the basis of your story will not differ greatly from other accounts. In this sense, the press conference is a particular challenge for the reporter. You must ask yourself: how can I get a different angle on this story?

Before you set out for the press conference, do some research into the subject and prepare a few questions. One way of making more of the story is to confront the interviewee with an unexpected question. Jot down at least four bullet points, which you would like to be covered. In other words, try to set your own agenda for the conference rather than being led by other journalists or those who have arranged the event.

Make sure you arrive early and get a seat at the front. If you do turn up late, do not sit at the back of the room; instead stand towards the front but at the side. The reason is that you need to be heard and interviewees are more likely to take questions from the front, rather than the back of the room.

Decide which is the most important of the four or five points that you have scribbled in your notebook and try to memorize a question along these lines. Because of the 'all-in' nature of press conferences, television and radio journalists tend to dominate the proceedings. They have the nearest deadlines so newspaper journalists often allow them the courtesy of getting their questions in first. Another reason is that experienced media performers, such as politicians, will search out television cameras at such events because the small screen is regarded as the most powerful news medium. Many would regard a 90-second spot on the Nine O'clock News infinitely superior to a page two news story in a high-circulation tabloid newspaper. A press conference also presents the television reporter with an opportunity to film some pictures, while the newspaper reporter does not have to consider the visual impact of the story.

At many press conferences, there will be a master of ceremonies, a sort of media minder who conducts the event. This person would be irrelevant apart from one important fact: they tend to choose which journalist is to ask the next question. You need to catch this person's eye before diving in with your question. If you are chosen, preface your first question with your name and newspaper as this may or may not make the interviewee sit up and notice.

Don't make your question too long. Asking a question in front of your peers can be potentially embarrassing but don't make matters worse by embarking on a long preamble setting out your pet theories on a particular subject. One short sentence is often enough. At a police news conference, you might ask: 'Are you confident of making an early arrest in this case?', 'Do you have any strong leads?' or 'How can the public help?'. And don't forget to speak loudly and clearly, as it will only irritate others if you need to repeat your question.

If you happen to mine a rich seam of newsworthy quotes, there is a convention which allows you to continue your line of questioning. This is a rarity, however, as every other journalist will also be keen to get their question in. When you first go to a news conference you may find it an intimidating event. There may be bright television lights, a large press corps and faces you might recognize. Try not to be put off by this and get your question in early. It will make you feel a lot more relaxed and allow you to concentrate on what is being said.

If you don't wish to ask your question/s during the actual conference, arrange with the PR/minder to interview the person after the presser is over in what is known as a 'separate'. This privilege is usually reserved for the broadcast media, but it can be the only way that you can guarantee that your angle on the story won't be reported by someone else. The disadvantage of revealing your great angle during the press conference is that everybody else will have the benefit of your analysis.

Take a small tape recorder with you to the press conference. Even if you are happy to take shorthand notes, a tape recorder is handy as a back-up and means you won't always be taking notes during what could be an hour-long conference. If you have arrived at the conference early, place the tape recorder on the desk or table at the front of the room where the questions will be answered. Some recorders now have an excellent range and this is not always necessary. But do not take any risks; you don't want to a miss a single quote, as that could be the story of the day. Having a tape recorder also allows you to take a note of the mood of the conference, which can be written into your story later as 'colour' or description to break up a long string of quotes. This helps the reader understand how the interviewee may be regarded by the press. For example, 'At a light-hearted press conference, so and so joked with the assembled media throng, showing a completely different side to his personality.'

Do not leave the conference before you are sure that you have everything you need to write your story. It will often happen that you are in a hurry to return to the newsroom, but before you do so glance back over your notes to make sure that you have all the pertinent news facts, such as who, what, where, when, why and how, that are crucial to the writing of any news story. If you haven't, approach the PR in charge of the news conference and ask for some details to be clarified. In most cases, once you have sat down to write the story back in the newsroom it will be too late to go over any points with the interviewee.

If you feel that you have completely missed the angle of the story at the news conference, chat to your fellow journalists afterwards. To many, this may seem unethical, clubbing together with other journalists to write up the same story. But really, all you are doing is 'standing up' your view of what has transpired at the conference. You do not have to reveal all that you think or what you feel the intro should be; simply share a few thoughts with the other writers and it could make the story perfectly clear to you. It is also helpful to hear what others have to say and how they intend to run the story. If a journalist from a rival paper intends to write it one way, you can simply do the opposite.

If it is possible, write your story immediately. It is often a good idea to think over a few different intros in your mind as you sit through some of the more uninteresting answers. Do not forget: you have the tape recorder as a back-up. If you have an opportunity, scribble down your first thoughts on an intro on the way back to the office, because the sooner you start to write your story the fresher it will be. There will be cases when you are simply providing quotes, which will be used in a story written by another journalist. If this is the case, you will need to file directly to copytakers down the phone by reading out your quotes from the notebook. This is where the tape recorder becomes a little useless. One of the other disadvantages of relying completely on a Dictaphone is that it is impossible to find quickly a quote that may have been made 20 minutes into the news conference.

The important factor to remember when writing up your story is that all your rivals have the same quotes to choose from (unless, of course you organized a separate interview). Because of this, make sure you think of an angle that is original, not necessarily the most obvious, but one that takes a slightly different approach to the subject. Try to recall an answer that seemed to provoke the most interest at the conference itself, using the other journalists as your 'members of the public'. Also, have a thought about what your readers would have asked the interviewee as this can often make you think of a more interesting intro.

Exercise 2: The press conference

You are the football reporter on *Mayfair and Kensington News*.You have been invited to a press conference by the Mayfair Football Club at their ground. It has been called to preempt a story that will appear in tomorrow morning's paper, connected with Mayfair manager Ronnie Campbell. A source tells you that the story is about a bribe paid to the manager before last year's FA Cup semi-final, which Mayfair lost. Prepare five questions to ask at the news conference.

(see page 135 for answers.)

Speeches

The second 'set piece' that you will find yourself covering as a reporter is the speech. In many ways, the motivation behind inviting the media to a speech is similar to a press conference: to control the message put across to the public. For many, the occasion itself is a very formal one, such as the Chancellor of the Exchequer's address at the Mansion House in the City. This 'event' is guaranteed to have press coverage and politicians will certainly have an eye to the calendar of set speeches whenever they decide it is appropriate to make a certain announcement.

One of the other advantages for the speechmaker is the sense of drama that an address can create. This is particularly relevant to television coverage, where speeches may be timed to coincide with news bulletins. As a newspaper reporter, your ability to create a sense of drama from the event will come from your descriptive abilities, by detailing how the speech was received by the audience.

Who makes speeches? Politicians mostly (on what is called the 'rubber chicken circuit', named after the delicious food served), but also business leaders and personalities (sporting and show business) on the 'after-dinner' circuit. The latter has become extremely popular and a far more lively proposition than being entertained by a junior minister outlining the latest plans for set-aside farming in the West Country.

Preparing to cover a speech involves a similar procedure to the news conference. Try to get there early, unless you have a reserved place at a table for a rubber chicken, in which case arrive a little later. If you do not have a reserved place, you will have a scramble for a seat with other journalists, but do try to get close to the podium if you wish to make a recording. The same equipment is required: notebook, a small tape recorder (not so essential as you should have a copy of a speech) and an iron-clad constitution.

One of the first things to do on arrival is speak to the PR people in charge of the event and make sure it is known who you are and which organization you represent. On most occasions you will be accosted as you come through the door, so eager are many PRs to pin one of those attractive plastic name tags on your jacket. Do not resist this attention: these tags often help to break the ice as you mingle among the guests after the speech to gauge reaction. As the name tag goes on, ask for the press pack that should include a copy of the speech and any accompanying press release. (Follow all previous instructions for handouts and bin it unless it looks vaguely interesting. It is normally how 'they' would like the speech to be written up. It can, however, point you towards an angle.)

Very considerate PRs might also refer you to specific passages in the speech that they feel contain the 'juicy bits'. In fact, some of the best PRs are ex-journalists. It's in their interest to get a good relationship with you – pointing to possible angles is a help. This 'direction' is often not far off the mark because most of the speech will be pitched at those present in the auditorium rather than a wider public. It also helps in structuring your story afterwards. You might think, having received such useful information before the speech has even been made, that there seems little reason to sit through the event itself. Apart from getting a free lunch or dinner, there often isn't. The danger of this, however, is that most speakers will depart from the written text at various points, leaving even the minders confused.

Listen carefully for the 'news' in the text. Try to think about what your readers might find interesting, as often what you find boring will also be of no consequence to anyone reading the piece. Ask yourself: why is the speaker saying this now and not simply issuing a press release next week? Try to pick out key words in the text that can point you towards a possible story. For example, phrases like 'The point I want to make', 'Let me make it quite clear', 'I urge you to' and 'Firstly, let me emphasize' should awaken you from your after-dinner/lunch slumber and be scribbled in your notebook.

It is advisable though to take only selective notes during speeches as you do not want to be forced to trawl through a mass of notes when compiling your story. Simply indicate the passages in the text that you may use later and make a further note yourself. Also, keep one eye on the advance copy of the speech so that you can identify whether the speaker has gone into a world of ad lib. Be ready to pounce on these: the shortest aside or throwaway line can often make a reasonable story. In particular, seize on any jokes as these can often mask a serious truth and make good copy in themselves. As most speakers will use an autocue together with a written speech, you will be able to see instantly when the speaker's eyes are trained directly on the audience. This is an especially good technique used by politicians for capturing the attention of a restless audience.

As with a press conference, observe how the audience is reacting to the speaker. Are they warming to the address? Is the speaker being heard in respectful silence? If you are sitting at a table, how are those sitting next to you receiving the message from the top table? And of course, talk to people afterwards. Was this the type of speech they were expecting to hear? Which parts of the address did they find the most interesting?

If you feel that the speaker has mentioned something very controversial and newsworthy, approach the PR about a quick post-speech interview to clarify any points. Often the PR can deal with these areas, but it can be helpful to get the speaker himself to explain in his own words what he was trying to say. And talk to other journalists to see if your view corresponds in any way with theirs; if it doesn't, go with your instincts and write up your own angle.

And a quick note on writing your story. Try to avoid a long string of quotes in your piece because this often reads like the speech itself. Break up the copy with plenty of references to the speaker, background to the story and any audience reaction. Given the nature of the event, you may even be entitled to a little analysis of the speech itself and the context in which it was delivered. When you are making these points, however, qualify any statements by using words such as 'seems', 'apparent', 'looks like', 'signalled'. These will make your judgements a little less definitive.

The vox pop

This is the English way of saying *vox populi*, which is Latin for the voice of the people. It is also known as a straw poll, so called because of the use of a piece of straw to show which way the wind was blowing. It was first coined in nineteenth century America, when journalists were sent to interview 'townsfolk' about how they intended to vote in a local election. It is a very effective way of keeping you and your readers in touch with what people are thinking about broader issues, such as sex, politics, social and moral questions. The vox pop is often used by local newspapers to give a national issue a local focus, but it is also used by national papers to take a snapshot of public opinion on a particular question. Vox pops also make for very entertaining copy as the general public are much more direct in their use of language than those more accustomed to making public statements.

The vox pop can take two forms: the structured or unstructured poll. In the first, you should list up to six questions on the main points of an issue. The advantage of this form of questionnaire is that the results can be compared with those from other reporters and a more conclusive analysis made. It is also possible to make certain predictions based on these results. Let us say the topic is the decriminalization of cannabis after a report from a leading politician saying decriminalization would benefit society. This is a perennial vox pop favourite.

First, prepare an opening statement. This is simply a sentence or two pointing out the reason for the survey. In this case, it may be 'In view of the widespread use of cannabis, its tacit acceptance by the police, possible medical benefits and calls for referenda on its use, should cannabis be legalized?'. Read this statement to each respondent before asking the survey questions so that they have a clear picture of the context.

Second, frame the questions so that the respondents are forced to answer 'yes/no/don't know'. Avoid open-ended questions demanding more complex answers because these are more difficult to compare with other responses. In the case of cannabis, your six questions could be: 'Have you taken cannabis?', 'Should cannabis be available on prescription?', 'Do you think the use of cannabis leads to hard drugs?', 'Do you think possession of small quantities of cannabis for personal use is acceptable?', 'Should cannabis be legalized?', 'Why?'.

The final question, 'Why', is what is known as a 'bucket question', where the aim is to receive a general response and a quote or two that you can use in your story. Do not rely too much on this type of question to give you an angle to your story because many members of the public will have to be pumped to express an opinion on many matters. They are also likely to be interviewed on the street where they might be in a hurry, so any response is unlikely to draw any wide-ranging conclusions.

If you are operating as a 'one-reporter' survey, the more people you question the better, but if you are one of a team agree a sample size at the start. Twenty should be about the minimum number of respondents to give a reasonable sample. Depending on the issue being canvassed, you may want to know other factors such as gender, salary and age, which can help to explain any conclusion that you make. For example, if you discover that the majority of people in favour of legalizing cannabis are women over 65 on a pension, this would be something of a revelation. Try not to be too fussy in your selection of respondents and approach people at random.

The unstructured survey is far less considered and normally involves an individual reporter being asked by the editor to interview a few people outside the office on a particular issue. It is obviously much less scientific. The aim is to find a few good quotes which represent the thinking of the man or woman 'on the Clapham omnibus' (traditionally seen as Mr and Mrs Average). Before you 'hit the pavement', frame a simple question that encapsulates the story, eg 'What is your view on the legalization of cannabis?' Approach as many people as you can – using a small tape recorder if you have one – and listen carefully to each response. If it begs another question, ask one but keep the interviews short. The aim is to provide the editor with a quick snapshot of public opinion, not an in-depth interview.

Exercise 3: The vox pop

Devise six questions, including a bucket question, based on the following topic about telethons.

Today is Comic Relief Day. We are doing a survey to find out people's attitudes towards televised fund raising. Telethons are becoming less effective in the ways they raise funds for charities.

Which six questions would you ask, remembering that they should not, excepting the last, result in an 'open' answer? (see page 135 for answers.)

Doorstops, all-ins and death knocks

Depending on your approach to journalism, these three confrontations are often necessary but not the most enjoyable. A doorstop interview is a very common tactic in which you plant yourself outside a building, from which you hope your interviewee will emerge. This can be their house or place of work, it doesn't matter. A doorstop often involves a long wait so be prepared to sit tight for some time and discuss the ills of the world with other journalists until your quarry appears. (It is always wise in these circumstances to refer to the PCC Code of Practice on Privacy which says that 'intrusions into an individual's private life are not generally acceptable unless it is in the public interest'.) Have a clear idea in your mind exactly what you would like the person to reveal as most doorstop interviews are comparatively brief affairs. Try to get your interviewee to answer this question and, if they won't do this, keep plugging away until they disappear into their car, which is often the case. Do not expect them to break away to offer you a separate interview because you represent a highly reputable national newspaper: it won't happen.

Given that the media tend to travel in packs, most doorstop interviews lead to an 'all-in' where several journalists converge on the interviewee in the manner of a rugby scrum. This is not intentional in most cases, but can become very uncomfortable if you find yourself caught in the middle (to say nothing for how the interviewee feels). For a newspaper reporter, the secret is to lay back slightly and allow your television and radio friends, because of their technological demands, to make the initial surge. If you are only using a notebook (not very advisable) you will also need space to scribble something down, unless of course 'No comment' is the answer you receive – a quite common result. Staying at the back of the pack also gives you the advantage of being able to pop a question or two once the interviewee breaks through the crowd. While you may receive an 'exclusive' word or two, it's inevitable that your colleagues will pump you for the result of any 'private' tête-à-tête.

The third confrontation, the 'death knock', is the worst duty you may ever have to carry out. If you are asked to interview the relatives of a victim, take a lead from the PCC Code of Practice, which states: 'In cases involving personal grief or shock, enquiries should be carried out and approaches made with sympathy and discretion.' Check that the relatives know of the death. It has been known for journalists to break the news before police arrive.

Most people are unlikely to want to discuss such stories over the telephone, so you will often find yourself going to a victim's house. If this is the case, and you are one of several journalists, appoint one person to negotiate an 'all-in' interview. Ask politely for a photograph if one is needed but do not lift one from the mantelpiece, as I have seen done, and bellow: 'Can we have this one, then?' The more tact used on these occasions, the better. Do not contribute to the stereotype of the unfeeling and cynical tabloid journalist who will stop at nothing to get a story.

4

News writing

Creating a news story

Writing a news story is the most fundamental skill you need to acquire as a journalist. Whether you find yourself working on a local freesheet, national title or in broadcast, your ability to turn a series of often quite uninteresting facts into a readable story will be most sought after.

Many journalists say that a good news story will simply write itself. On the face of it, this statement is nonsense, but it does have a grain of truth. The reporter who sits down to write a 300-word piece on a fire at a local bed and breakfast will need to understand fully in his mind 'what the story is about' before keying a single word into the terminal. As soon as he does, the story may indeed write itself. Therefore the more obvious the story is in the mind of the journalist, the easier it is to write.

Speed and accuracy will be crucial to your success in news writing. In a newsroom environment you may sometimes have less than 20 minutes, depending on the individual newspaper, to work on a story before it needs to be sent to the news editor. There are many reasons why you may have so little time to work on a piece. The main one is that you are the first step in the editorial process. As we know, after the story leaves your screen it needs to be read by editors, sub-editors and finally the paper's editor, before it ends up on the printed page. All of these people may want to put their own 'spin' on the story or rewrite it.

One danger, however, in writing a story quickly is inaccuracies. As you are writing the piece always refer to your notes to make sure the right facts are going into the story. Some reporters also choose to talk again to those people that they have interviewed to verify their notes.

Let us take the example of a fatal accident on the high street. Often when reporting on these incidents your first port of call will be the local police station. The police can be a good source of information on many issues, not just those related to crime. Once you have written your story, you may discover that a certain fact doesn't ring true with the rest of the piece. It may be one of several things: the age of the driver, the victim's injuries, how many people were in the car at the time, which way along the street the car was travelling.

All these minor pieces of information, that make up the fabric of the copy, can become muddled in the process of notetaking or writing. Do not be afraid to ring the sergeant and/or press relations officer to double check the information. It reflects badly on you as a professional if the facts which appear in the paper are wrong. Not only is such a mistake embarrassing for you and the newspaper, but it can also be costly. The printing of an apology for the smallest oversight takes up time and valuable space in the paper. The reader would much prefer to see a news story on the page, than an apology. Striking the right balance between speed and accuracy may be difficult to achieve in the early stages of your career so it is best to get the story right. Journalists often joke that the facts should never get in the way of a good story – don't let this be your epitaph.

The structure of a news story

Let us look at the pyramid concept (Figure 1), which forms the backbone of a well-written story. Many journalists may not realize that they are writing to this formula, but if you analyse most stories you will discover that they all conform to this general shape. However, don't expect to hear reporters in a newsroom asking each other what is at the top of their respective pyramids. Most experienced journalists find writing an automatic, instinctive process and do not dwell on ideas such as the pyramid. You will find, too, that as you write more stories, you start to go through this process automatically yourself, deciding first on an angle, then an intro, before writing the remainder of the story.

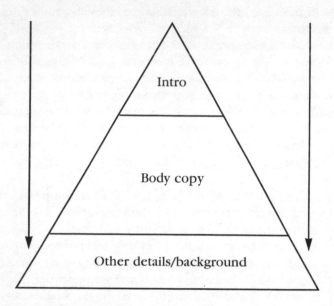

Figure 1 *News pyramid*

The pyramid, a simple triangle in effect, shows the structure of a news story, from the intro or lead at the top to other details/background at the base (Figure 1). When writing a news story we start from the top of the pyramid, not the bottom. So, why use a pyramid? Unlike other forms of writing, such as short stories or novels, news stories tend to begin with the 'result' of the event or incident rather than what may have happened first. If you were writing a short story you would probably end with a climax of some sort by building your narrative to an appropriate ending. With a news story, however, your climax comes at the top of the copy, or the top of the pyramid.

Next stop on your descent of the pyramid is the main body copy, which includes any background to the story and the most relevant facts that you have gathered. Again this is a process of assembling quotes (ie direct speech from someone you have interviewed, such as 'I saw the car round the bend, then collide with the lamp-post. It was terrible') and pieces of description from the writer.

The base of your pyramid is other details/background. These are primarily the pieces of information that you feel are less important because they fail to add any more to the interest value of the story. Writing a news story is a sifting process where you include some facts but throw away others. In the bottom third of the pyramid, you will often find information that doesn't materially add to your understanding of the story. In short, it is superfluous. In the case of the fatal car accident on the High Street, this might include a further eyewitness account that is similar to other accounts. It might be the fact that the lamp-post was one of the best examples of its kind to be found in the county, and will be irreplaceable. If one particular fact prompts you to ask, 'So what?', there is every reason to think that a reader will have the same reaction.

Always remember: writing a news story is a progression from the most important facts to the least important. The idea is to start from the top of the pyramid and work your way down. If you scale it from the bottom, the reader's attention will be lost by end of the third paragraph. Let's look at two typical news stories from *The Express*. The first of these appeared on page two. The headline read:

Miner feared dead in roof collapse horror

A coal miner was feared dead last night after being trapped in a roof collapse which also injured three other workers.

Rescue experts were spearheading a recovery operation at the Castle Drift Mine at Blenkinsopp near Haltwhistle, Northumberland, but there was little hope of the man being found alive. He was trapped among more than 30 tonnes of rubble over a mile from the entrance when a limestone slab crushed roof supports.

One miner has back injuries, one chest injuries and one leg injuries. Police said the recovery operation might not be completed until later today.

This story appeared at the bottom of the page, which indicates that it was viewed as less important than others on the same page. It may also have been placed there because it was a late-breaking piece and could be accommodated easily into this space. It is a short news story, only three paragraphs in length, but the essence of what has happened to the coal miner is captured in the intro.

Here we are told that a coal miner is feared dead in a roof collapse – the most important fact in the story. One of the best ways to decide on an intro is to imagine that you are explaining what has happened to a friend or colleague. In many cases this is exactly what you would tell the news editor if you had just heard the news your-self. You would simply say that there has been a roof collapse at a mine and a coal miner is feared dead. Think of the top of the pyra-mid again. The most important fact in this story is the feared death of the coal miner. In other words, it is the 'result' of what has hap-pened in the mine collapse, not an explanation of what happened.

There is, however, another important fact mentioned in the intro-duction – it is that three other miners were injured in the roof col-lapse. It is often said that there is never a right or wrong way to write a story and this illustrates the point perfectly. For an intro, the journalist could have written: 'Three coal miners were injured and another feared dead last night when a roof collapsed at a mine in Northumberland.'

In my reworked lead, I have given slightly more emphasis to the three injured miners. It is unlikely that you would ever write an intro to such a story that would give prominence to those that were injured above any reported deaths. This second version does, how-ever, give the reader a better sense of the scale of the collapse. The location of the mine is also mentioned, an important fact that read-ers should know quite early in the story.

In the next paragraph the reader is given more details about the story. This is the *body copy* and *background* in the pyramid struc-ture. In this part of the story we are told that rescue experts have gone to the scene of the mine at Haltwhistle in Northumberland. Should you have been writing a later version of this story you may have 'renosed' (if asked to renose a story by your editor, it means writing a new intro) the story by saying: 'Rescue workers were last night trying to free a coal miner feared dead in a roof collapse in Northumberland.'

We are then told that there is little hope of finding the miner alive, bearing out the first line of the intro. It is crucial that definitive statements made in the copy are backed by a quote or explanation later in the story. We can assume, in this instance, that the reporter has spoken to someone at the mine who has held out little hope that the miner will survive the ordeal.

The next sentence is relevant background to the tragedy. It appears that the most seriously injured man was 'trapped among more than 30 tonnes of rubble over a mile from the entrance when a limestone slab crushed roof supports'. This sentence is critical to

our understanding of the man's plight. It also bears out the assertion
that there is little hope of finding the miner alive. In a much longer
piece, where more detail is known, these facts may well have
formed the bulk of the introduction. Here is an alternative way of
writing the intro to emphasize the difficulty of the man's fight for
survival. 'A man was fighting for his life under 30 tonnes of rubble
last night after a roof collapse at a mine in Northumberland.'

On a grammatical note, you may have noticed that the story is
written in the past tense, ie 'A coal miner *was* feared dead last night'
as opposed to the present tense that would have read 'A coal miner
is feared dead', ignoring any reference to the time of day. Past tense
or past continuous are the dominant styles for news stories in most
newspapers. When we come to look at features, there is greater
scope for different writing styles. This is not to say that all news stories must be written in the past tense. If you preview an event that
is due to happen the following day or month, the present tense
would be better. Do not forget: there are no fixed stylistic rules; rules
will generally be dictated by the publication concerned. In this case,
it is *Express* style to write most news stories in the past tense. When
you join a publication or want to write freelance for a certain title,
study its style before submitting any work. It will also help you
understand how style works.

Let's move on to the third and final paragraph. Admittedly this is
a short news story, no more than a hundred words, but it does conform loosely to the pyramid structure. One reason why stories are
written with the most important facts at or towards the top of the
copy is that space in a newspaper is at a premium. Sub-editors, who
receive your copy to cut into the page, tend to edit the story from
the bottom of the text so, by including what you consider to be the
most crucial facts in the first few sentences, you ensure, in most
cases, that these details will survive.

The story now describes the injuries to the other three miners:
one has chest injuries, one has back injuries, one has leg injuries.
These are details that the story could have done without. While it
does help the reader to understand the seriousness of the injuries,
it fails to take the story much further. It may have been more helpful to the reader to have known the extent of the injuries to the
most seriously hurt miner, but this is obviously not known at this
stage.

In the final sentence the police tell us that the recovery operation might not be completed until later today. While this element of the story is of some interest to the reader, it is not imperative to our understanding of the roof collapse. It does indicate in a small way that the collapse is considerable because it will take quite some time to rescue the injured miners. It is fair to say that this final sentence could be deleted without altering the main thrust of the story. Here we come across one of the rules for keeping some facts in a story while discarding others: if a fact does not add to your under standing or interest in the story, get rid of it.

The next *Express* story that we will look at appeared in the same edition on page five. It was headlined:

I'm blameless says detective

A retired detective blamed over the case of the Bridgewater Three last night denied fabricating evidence.

Former Detective Constable Graham Leake insisted that he never took part in forging a confession which led to the conviction of the men.

His solicitors issued a statement saying they do not believe there is any evidence which would support charges against Mr Leake or his former colleagues.

Mr Leake was one of three ex-policemen named last week when Michael Hickey, Vincent Hickey and James Robinson were released from jail pending an appeal against their conviction for the murder of newspaper boy Carl Bridgewater.

The High Court decided that evidence used in their 1979 trial had been fabricated by police. Earlier yesterday West Midlands Chief Constable Edward Crew admitted at the time of the case it was normal for officers to interrogate suspects before they even bothered to look for further evidence.

When asked if interrogations could get 'rough', Mr Crew 'replied: Of course, they could.'

Mr Robinson yesterday appealed on TV for the Bridgewater family to believe him when he said he did not kill their son.

'God love your child, it wasn't us,' he said.

This story is a follow-up piece to the reporting of the Bridgewater Three case the previous week. The intro very succinctly tells the reader the nub of the story: 'A retired detective blamed over the case of the Bridgewater Three last night denied fabricating evidence.'

This is all the reader needs to know in the first paragraph, capitalizing on a well reported story and revealing a new, important development. The intro also illustrates perfectly the pyramid idea: the most important fact has taken its place at the top of the story. Note that the story does not begin with an account of the murder of Carl Bridgewater, which would have been the angle when the story was first reported. The reason is that you must assume that in a running story (ie a story that has been reported before) the reader will have some background knowledge. The shortage of space in newspapers does not allow you to repeat all the background of 'old' stories. If disaster struck the printing of this page and the rest of the story failed to print, readers would still understand the new development – given their assumed knowledge of the story.

This intro shows how well simplicity works and, by not including any pertinent details at this point, such as the detective's name, the reader is left wanting to know more. Had such information been included in the first sentence, the lead would have been a slower. A 'fast' intro is one that the reader can digest quickly. The second paragraph takes us into *body copy* in our pyramid e. It tells us immediately the identity of the former policeman, perhaps the most important fact in the piece. In a longer story, a trimmed second sentence may well have been included in the action. The third paragraph takes us back, in effect, to the timing of the story, ie how do we come to know this revelation? Paragraph four is all background. In most news stories of this length it should be possible for a writer to summarize any background in one paragraph. In this instance the next sentence reveals more details, telling us that the High Court 'decided that evidence used in their 1979 trial had been fabricated by police'. The remainder of this paragraph tells the reader of an earlier development in day involving the West Midlands Chief Constable Edward Crew. Note how the story has now moved on to a completely different angle. Why wasn't the statement of the chief constable more important than that of Mr Leake's solicitors?

One reason is that it happened earlier in the day and it may have already been covered by other media, and secondly, the Leake statement is the first by one of the police officers involved in the case. A choice has been made by the writer or editor to run the solicitor's statement at the top of the story, ahead of the admisions by the chief constable. The reason is that many readers will already have heard the news relating to the chief constable.

The next paragraph is partly a direct quote from the chief constable, taken from an interview. Direct quotes are used in stories to add weight and validity. If the reader sees a quote from someone involved in the incident it adds to the story's integrity. When a direct quote cannot be used because of space, the person will be paraphrased. This gives an essence of what has been said and, in many cases, means that more of the substance of the interview will make it into the paper. Quotes also look better in a story, as they break up long pieces of dense looking copy.

The final two paragraphs can definitely be assigned to *other details* on the bottom layer of our pyramid. They deal with a third facet of the story: an appearance on television of one of the Bridgewater Three, James Robinson. Not only did this appear on television, but it happened much earlier in the day so is less important.

The Leake piece is a good example of how three separate developments are handled in one story: a solicitor's statement on behalf of Mr Leake, a comment by the chief constable Edward Crew and a television statement by one of the Bridgewater Three, James Robinson. Two of these have less importance because they are 'old news'. Both the Robinson and Crew statements may already have been picked up by readers during the day from television or radio, but the Leake statement was made the previous night. More importantly though, the Leake development will have a bearing on where the story goes from here and it is crucial to our understanding of why the Bridgewater Three have been released from jail pending their appeal. The Leake statement therefore is the most important, the Robinson TV appearance the least important.

Choosing an angle

Given the ever present deadlines in news writing, it is critical that while you are involved in gathering the necessary information for the story, you are also thinking of a possible angle. The angle of a story is the approach the journalist takes to the story. Let us say that you have gathered some information over the phone on that car accident on the local high street, which we discussed earlier. (It may sound banal but it is a common story that is covered by journalists on regional newspapers.) Road accidents happen all the time, so the secret is to unlock a certain piece of information or fact that will become what we call the 'angle' for your story.

We have already talked about the nature of news and central to this is the angle, which only on rare occasions will jump out of the copy. On the face of it, a fatal accident in the high street does not always make a news story. If in your news gathering you discover that the driver was trapped in the wreckage for 90 minutes before being freed by a special new device, this might be an angle. If it turns out that this special device has only recently been introduced for use by the local police force, it is an even better story. If you discover nothing of the sort, it becomes just another fatal accident, and is worth perhaps one or two paragraphs.

To many this may sound callous and cynical. Why, you may ask, not just concentrate on the fact that someone was killed? You will be forced to make choices such as this throughout your journalism career and they are not easy. Always ask yourself: what would the reader find interesting about this story? What questions would a reader ask someone about the incident?

You may already have appreciated that both news gathering and news writing involve a series of choices. First there is the choice of whether a particular piece of information makes a news story. That decided, you must choose the most important facts about the story, which will then constitute the introduction. Having written the introduction, you must then decide which are the most relevant facts for the body of the story. Choices upon choices: make the right ones and you will have a good piece of copy.

So, we have now chosen our angle: it is that the driver, who happens to have survived this terrible crash, was rescued with the use of a special piece of equipment, sometimes called the 'jaws of life'. With this angle we can start to think about writing the first and most important part of a news story: the intro.

Writing the intro

Why is the intro, sometimes called the lead, so important? One of the joys of getting your news from a newspaper is that you can read it, if you have time, at a leisurely pace. As you turn the pages, you can dip into a story, read a little, skim read another piece or simply glance at the headlines and move on. In most instances, however, the reader will first digest the opening sentence of the story – the introduction. While we can't be certain about how people read newspapers, it would be reasonable to say that most people read the opening sentence of most stories on a particular page, either choosing to read on or go to another page. Next time you are reading the papers with someone else take note of the way in which they scan the page for something interesting.

As a news writer it is your job to grab the interest of this reader immediately. By writing a good intro, you not only absorb the reader, encouraging them to read further on into the story, but also clarify the essence of the story in your own mind. On any news page you are competing for space with other stories and other writers, so a good, simply written introduction will do much to keep the reader's eye on your story and not someone else's. Journalism is a team game but some healthy competition does not go astray.

> **TIP:**
> A good intro grabs the attention of the reader and keeps it there.

Who, what, where, when, why and how?

What information should be included in the introduction? There are six facts that must, in whole or part, be included in the lead and they are *who, what, where, when, why and how.* This is perhaps the most important rule to learn in writing news stories because not only does it help the reader digest immediately the most pertinent facts, but it assists the reporter in gathering the most relevant information about the story. If, in the case of our car accident, you are talking to the police, it will help you to collect all these facts before deciding whether you have a story. Should any one of these facts strike you as being remotely interesting, you may have a story worth reporting. Otherwise, pass on to the next item.

The *who* fact is self-evident, dealing with the identity of the subject of the story. In our fatal car accident, it would normally be the fatality of the crash. However, because we have chosen to pursue another angle– the victim who escaped the wreckage because of the 'jaws of life' – he would be the *who* fact. When you come to write your story you may have several *who* facts: it is your job to choose the one that makes the strongest story. Always think: how can I grab the reader's attention? Would I be interested in reading a story about this? Would my friends?

If you have time, ask yourself these questions and it will help you arrive at the most interesting angle. The *who* fact can also be an organization or even an animal. In our two *Express* stories, the *who* facts were the coal miner and the retired detective.

The *what* fact is a little more difficult to grasp. The best way to think about it is to ask yourself: *what* happened? In our car accident, the *what* fact involves the rescue of a man using the jaws of life. In general terms, it is often the *result* of the story that becomes the *what* fact. If you do not have a *what* fact, I am afraid you do not have a story. Something must have happened to someone or something in order for there to be a newsworthy event. In the two *Express* stories, the *what* facts are, in the first, that the coal miner *is feared dead in a roof collapse*; in the second it is that the retired detective *has denied fabricating evidence.*

The *who* and *what* facts are the two most important facets of the intro. The other four may be left until the second paragraph, but these two aspects will immediately involve your readers and encourage them to read on. Often the best intros are those written for news briefs when journalists are faced with coming up with only a few words to tell an entire story. Usually an intro is only one sentence, but sometimes two or three sentences may be needed to get the story across, such as in the case of a complex political story. A rule of thumb, certainly for a tabloid newspaper or a regional paper, is to keep the intro to just one single sentence; a broadsheet paper may use two.

The Detective Leake story that appeared in *The Express* is a perfect example of a short, concise intro that encapsulates the latest development. The reader knows straight away what the story is about with the mention of a key phrase, ie 'the Bridgewater Three; and it outlines new information, ie the ex-detective has denied fabricating evidence.

> **TIP:**
> Keep it simple and don't bombard the reader with too much
> information, too soon.

The *when* fact should be obvious. Literally, it is '*when* did the
event happen?' In the case of the roof collapse and the former
detective, it is the previous night. It is common practice for this fact
to appear in the first paragraph. It informs the reader that you are
up to date with the story and are following developments. You may
sometimes notice that the *when* fact is absent. This can be for several reasons, but most notoriously when the story is an old one and
a paper wishes to disguise the fact that they have only just received
the news. If the story is old, the *when* fact will be buried in the
fourth or fifth paragraph. Newspapers, while losing the battle of
immediacy to radio and TV, are still in the business of providing the
latest angles and this is worth emphasizing in your story. If it happened late last night and your paper has managed to get the story
before the final edition, say so.

The *where* fact is again quite obvious. *Where* did the story happen? That is, what is the location? In the story about ex-Detective
Leake you may notice that this fact is missing. The reason is that the
where fact is not crucially important to our understanding of the
story. It isn't necessary for us to say that the statement made by Mr
Leake was issued from a solicitor's office in the West Midlands.
Better to save on space and include another more interesting detail.
In the roof collapse, the opposite is the case. The reader will want
to know the *where* fact more than perhaps any other piece of information. Every story is different and thus the formula for writing it
will differ in each case. Do not just include the *where* fact for the
sake of it. In a local newspaper, the *where* fact is very important as
readers will be very concerned about what is happening on their
doorstep. After all, this is why they have bought it. You will notice,
therefore, that local papers can be very parochial, often including
street numbers, even house names, when identifying someone in a
story. The opposite is so on national papers where you might find
that the *where* fact is 'fudged' a little, especially if the story is about
some bizarre event in the American Midwest. People read different
papers for different reasons: one motivation for buying a national

title is not to discover what may be happening on your own doorstep, even though certain stories may affect you in some way.

The *why* fact is optional in many stories. If, for instance, you are writing a piece about a hurricane there is no point attempting to explain why a hurricane occurs because it is an act of nature. But in the story of the coal miner the reader will be very interested in the *why* fact because this has implications for the future safety of the mine. For ex-Detective Leake, the *why* fact is less interesting. Indeed, a *why* fact of sorts is found in the fifth paragraph: 'The High Court decided that evidence used in their 1979 trial had been fabricated by police.' Mr Leake is obviously responding to this accusation, borne out by what we call the 'caption bullet' below the picture which reads: 'ACCUSED'. Try to avoid the *why* fact if you believe it is self-evident to the reader. Use this valuable space for something else.

The *how* fact, often very similar to the *why* fact, is the most mysterious element in the introduction. Essentially, it only applies to certain stories where we are interested in a particular process. It can also apply to how the journalist actually came to have the story in the first place. However, in the Leake story, we are not so concerned with how the statement was issued, whether it was by fax or carrier pigeon, though if it was the latter it might be worth putting in. In the roof collapse story, the *how* fact is very important. It doesn't warrant inclusion in the intro but it does make it into the second paragraph: 'when a limestone slab crushed roof supports'. In the case of the fatal car accident, it is equally important as the reader will want to know how the accident happened; indeed the phrase 'The accident happened when' is often used.

Here is your *intro checklist*:

1. Does it give the NEWS as you would tell it to your own news editor?
2. Can a good headline be written from it?
3. Is it a 'potted' version of the whole story, which could be published on its own?
4. Does it present the most important or most interesting points of the story?
5. Do the first six or seven words present a fact that would attract the attention of a hasty reader?

6. Is the sentence structure simple enough for a reader to grasp the meaning at a glance?
7. Is it the right length – between 18 and 30 words?

What to avoid:

1. Never start with a date.
2. Avoid starting with a name, unless the person is well known.
3. Do not use 'long' words. Keep it simple.
4. Do not use too many adjectives.

Exercise 1:

Identify the *who*, *what* and *when* facts in the following intros.

1. The Archbishop of York, John Habgood, called today for tax cuts for married people to support the family. He says current policies treat cohabiting couples as if they were married, so they see no advantage in getting married.

Here is some help for the first one: *who,* Archbishop of York John Habgood; *what,* calls for tax cuts for married people; *when,* today.

2. A woman police officer was raped by a male colleague after a 'toffs and tarts' New Year party, the Old Bailey heard yesterday.

3. A wealthy Tory activist was shot dead by his son after nagging him for years about his lack of intelligence and low achievement, an inquest was told yesterday.

4. Diane Blood raised a glass of champagne last night as she cleared the last major hurdle in her fight to have a baby using her dead husband's sperm.

5. The Russian Defence Ministry announced last night it had reached a deal with the head of the Chechen forces to stop using heavy weapons after five hours of talks in a border village in Ingushetia.

(see page 136 for answers.)

Exercise 2:

Here is your chance to write your first intro. Read through the following details that you have gathered for a story. Make a list of *who*, *what*, *when*, etc, facts and write away.

The National Lottery draw on Saturday produced ten winners from a syndicate. The total jackpot was £20m. Each person in the syndicate will receive £2m.

One person from the syndicate, Joe Campbell, a kitchen hand, said: 'The first thing I'm going to do is buy a big bottle of champagne and drink it all. Then I'll get a new car, probably a Merc.'

All ten people in the syndicate worked at a restaurant in Sydenham, London. The chef, Graham Walsh, said: 'It's going to change my life. I can't wait to get my hands on the money and stop working.'

The owner of the restaurant, Margaret Riding, who also shared in the jackpot, said: 'I'm going to have to close the restaurant because I won't have any staff.'

Several regular customers said they were very concerned about the closure because it was the only decent restaurant in the area.

Customer Mrs Betty Jones said: 'I really don't know what I'm going to do on Saturday nights if they close this place.'

Two examples of how you might write an intro to this story can be found in the answers on page 136.

Structuring your story

We have now reached the second most important part of the news story pyramid. Having written the intro, your job now is to structure the remaining facts to form the body copy.

This part is primarily guided by what you consider to be the most interesting information in front of you. In this respect you have an editorial role in selecting some details but excluding others. However, this is where such a role begins and ends. It must be stressed that your job in writing a news story is to tell the truth, the whole truth and nothing but the truth.

Many journalists often make the mistake of treating a news story like an editorial. Do not fall into this trap or you will come unstuck. Be objective and assemble the facts, not your own opinions, in a logical sequence. On the face of it, this may sound like rather a dry exercise, but later in your career you may have the opportunity to express your opinion about certain issues. We will look at the ways this is done in feature writing in Chapter 6.

One other important reason for resisting the temptation to give your opinion is the danger of libel or contempt of court. In the *Express* story concerning ex-Detective Leake, an inexperienced reporter could easily be led to comment on a case that was still the subject of an appeal. It is also a little arrogant to believe that the reader would like to hear your opinion on a particular story. While newspapers tend to have a stronger editorial line than, say, television news, they are not an automatic platform from which to express your views. In writing your report, it is your role to judge what is newsworthy and of importance to the reader from the information you have gathered. Of course, it is impossible to be totally objective as you do this, but it should be your goal.

While having put a bit of a dampener on opinionated journalism, it should be said that writing objectively does not stop you developing your own writing style. To many people, style is an elusive concept, but it is possible to develop it during your career. Learn how to write a good news story and your style will grow over time as you become more confident.

The most efficient way to 'prioritize' the raw data is to read through each quote or fact that you have collected and rank them in order of importance, say from one to ten. If you have several different sources, for example you have interviewed three different eyewitnesses, rank these in a similar way. By doing this you will automatically structure your story. It can be as simple as this.

As you scan your quotes make sure that each new fact that you intend using takes the story a little further, but is linked in some way. Do not have two eyewitness accounts, for example, retelling a similar description of the same incident. Even though the language might differ, the substance will be the same and repetitive for the reader. Remember: always bear the reader in mind.

Try to maintain the interest factor as you collate your story by taking a slightly different angle on the incident, perhaps including an offbeat quote. You will find that many stories you write will be about similar subjects, so finding inspiration can sometimes be difficult.

During this sifting process, you may discover that many pertinent facts are missing in your story. If you have time you will need to return to your sources or interviewees and go back over the facts. If by chance they don't know or can't reveal what you wish to know, leave the information out of the story. Do not include any fact about which you are not certain. Check, check, check! Trust and reliability are bywords for getting on in the world of newspapers and it is often better to be known for these two attributes than for being a stylish writer.

Many shorter news stories will not include any quotes at all, as in the case of the roof collapse piece in *The Express*. The bulk of the body copy here is narrative – the writer is telling a story, as opposed to quoting someone else. As you 'tell the story' make sure that you are answering the *who, what, where, when, why* and *how* facts. As mentioned earlier, it is unlikely that any intro will cover all these points, but most will need to be dealt with eventually, otherwise the reader will be left asking the questions.

You may discover that you can simply write the story in a chrono-logical order. This is the most straightforward structure and lends itself to crime stories, court reports, sports, even a House of Commons story. Of course, every story has a chronology, but often you will need to take a different angle, such as in the Detective Leake story, so that you will not be covering old ground.

Let's look at the structure of this story that appeared on page 16 of *The Express:*

Couple who found teenage music a moving experience

Parents of a teenager whose pounding jungle music drives neighbours wild have decided to sell up and move home.

John and Patricia Barber can no longer afford to pay for their son's anti-social taste in music – having been hit with their second £2,700 penalty in just seven months.

Schoolboy John-Paul Barber, 16, made headlines last July when his parents were ordered to pay the huge fine and costs after upsetting neighbours with his late-night music.

But he continued to turn up the volume while his parents were out making their neighbour Denise Graham's flat shake, Haringey magistrates heard yesterday.

After being told to pay a massive penalty, John-Paul's parents have decided enough is enough and will move from their £100,000 flat in Muswell Hill, north London, rather than risk further fines.

'We should be grateful that John-Paul's worst vice is playing music too loud,' said Mr Barber, who runs a car hire business.

'He wants to be a disc jockey when he leaves school so maybe one day he can pay me back.'

He added: 'I know it's my fault for not being able to control him but short of throwing him out of the house, as no father could, I don't know what I am supposed to do.'

The intro tells the story of a couple who have decided to sell up and move home because their teenage son's loud music is costing them too much in fines.

The second paragraph fleshes out some detail in the case, giving you the parents' names, the latest amount that their son has been fined and the time span of the case. So far the story has dealt with half of the *who* (John and Patricia Barber), the *what* (forced to move house), the *why* (because of their son's loud music) but has not covered the *where* or *when* or *how*.

This is a classic case of a lighter court story, in which some of the important detail, such as where the family live, can be put lower in the story so that the essence of their dilemma can be outlined in the first two paragraphs. And given that this is a national newspaper, the location of the house in London is not important.

It is not until the third paragraph that we actually see the rest of the *who* fact (the boy's name and age, John-Paul Barber, 16) and the reporter outlines the background to the case. The story is told chronologically, detailing how the court first fined the boy back in July after he upset the neighbours with his loud music.

It is in the next paragraph that we learn that the latest development happened yesterday (the *when*), when the case was heard before Haringey magistrates (the *where*). We have now covered all the essential facts in the story with the possible exception of the location of the Barber's house. This detail comes in paragraph five, which reiterates the crux of the story: the Barbers deciding that 'enough is enough'. This is important. It takes the reader back to the intro of the story, reinforcing the angle (what the story is about) and providing a little more context by suggesting it was this latest fine which finally made the parents decide to move.

In the three remaining paragraphs we find out *how* the story has surfaced. It is highly unlikely that during the court proceedings the couple would have told the magistrates that they would be forced to move house. What has happened is that Mr Barber has been interviewed by a reporter outside the court and these three quotes are the result.

Notice how the first quote simply appears, without any introduction. For example, it doesn't say, 'Here is Mr Barber, who said:'. This sort of preamble would take up too much space and allow you less room for direct speech. Don't forget: let the facts tell the story. For the greatest impact then, begin with the quote itself, cold. It will interest the reader, especially if the person quoted has been already mentioned in the story. If the person has not, you could construct it like this: 'Mr John Barber, the boy's father, said outside the court: 'We should be grateful.'

In the second to last or penultimate paragraph we gain a greater insight into why the son continued to play the music, even though the family was liable to be fined again. This fact could have gone higher in the story, perhaps in the third paragraph, where the boy's name is first mentioned. The quote also shows us the extent of the problem faced by the parents in this case, and this is further illustrated in the final paragraph.

The device 'He added' is often used in copy, together with 'He continued'. They both indicate to the reader a continuation of the same subject and interviewee. It also breaks up the flow of quotes and, as a rule, you should avoid using more than three consecutive quotes. Keep the reader engaged at all times by taking the story in different directions, as has happened here. In this story, when it appears that we have reached a natural conclusion, we read some quotes from the father which take the piece on to a new tack.

Another good aspect to the structure of this story is that, had the editor wished to cut this piece, for whatever reason, it could have been done with little fuss by simply lopping off the last three paragraphs.

There are several other points to remember when using quotations. You are quite within your rights to paraphrase a quote or quotes if you feel they are too long or don't sufficiently outline a point that could have been made better. If you are going to paraphrase, simply preface the information with the interviewee's name, then use reported speech (for example, Mr Barber said that it was a very good thing, etc).

One contentious journalistic debate is the degree to which one is allowed to change what appears in the quote. Strictly speaking, a quote should go into print as it appeared in your notes, ie verbatim. However, this happens less than it should for two reasons. Often, the pressures of time and space dictate that they must be changed. It is better to run two short quotes to explain fully an issue rather than one long quote that doesn't.

Another point of debate is whether it is right to leave words in a quote that may make the interviewee seem ridiculous, even stupid. This will depend on the publication for which you are working. If you are a reporter on a national newspaper it is unlikely that they will have such a policy. They will usually try to make a quote understood, so you are right to add the odd word or two to improve meaning. An incomprehensible quote is no help to anyone.

When you are faced with a decision about whether to use a quote or paraphrase, I would always suggest the former. Try to let the people tell the story, for even though you may feel you can say it better, the story will read better with more quotes. It also helps the reader understand the attitude of the person interviewed.

Story checklist

1. Has the intro passed the intro writing test?
2. Is the story constructed so that it amplifies the points you have made in the intro, one by one, in order of importance?
3. Has the story answered the six basic questions: *who*, *what*, *when*, *where*, *why* and *how*?
4. Have you checked the names, titles, ages and addresses of the *who* characters?
5. Is the *when* of the story up-to-date, ie today, yesterday, etc? Do not forget that you will be writing for either the next day, the next Sunday, the next week (on a local paper) or next month, so try to keep it as urgent as possible.
6. Is it factual? Have you included the necessary attribution (ie according to so-and-so)?
7. Is it objective? Your story should not tell the reader what you

think or believe, *only what you know to be fact*.
8. Delete over-vivid verbs, adjectives and adverbs.
9. Does the story flow? Remember that a good news story should tell itself.
10. Is the background (ie non-narrative) information in the right place – either backing up the intro briefly, or towards the end after the narrative?
11. Has it been written so that it can be cut from the end without losing any important facts?
12. Have you avoided beginning with a quote?

Running stories and breaking news

One of the news stories we looked at from *The Express*, the statement by ex-Detective Leake, is described as a 'running story'. This means that this is the latest episode in a story which started some time ago.

In the case of the Leake statement, it is not necessary to involve the reader in all the previous happenings. We must assume that the public has some knowledge of the case. If we did not, most stories would run to ridiculous lengths and never cover anything new.

Breaking news happens when a story is unfolding before you. This is more relevant to radio and television, but you may find yourself on a newspaper shift when an event is happening over several hours. The most common examples are train and plane crashes, fires, storms, volcanoes and other natural disasters. They are 'breaking' because information about them tends to come in dribs and drabs. This is either because it is difficult to discover what has happened or because the story itself is still unfolding.

Here are some points to remember. When writing a breaking news story, you must always find a new angle to update your intro. This may mean some rewriting but you may be able keep sections of the body copy and background and write around it. Try to structure the story chronologically as this will not only make it easier to write but also inject drama. Have an eye to what may happen in the future. If a rescue is going on in a coal mine, for instance, look ahead to the next development: the enquiry, the causes.

Exercise 3:

Here is one further news writing exercise. Write a full-length story based on the following information for a local newspaper. Remember to cover all the main points in the intro.

> Firemen were called to a house in south London. It is in Waley St in Carshalton and it is 4am in the morning on Sunday.
> Police have said there are three people inside the small terrace house, which has two bedrooms upstairs.
> Eyewitness Terry Brigg: 'The firemen arrived about 4.15am. It woke us up. It's really good that they got those people out. I get on the same bus as that bloke.'
> Fire officer William Green said: 'The flames have a hold on the building. We are trying to get the people out.'
> Eyewitness Walter Seaman lives across the road: 'I just heard this explosion, raced outside and saw the house go up. I think the Walshs live there.'
> Fireman David Pascoe said: 'I managed to get the parents out first, Jill and Tony, but couldn't find their young baby Daniel anywhere.'
> 'I looked everywhere. Finally I found him under a wardrobe in the bedroom. The blast had been so strong that he had been blown under there. It was just luck that I found him.'
> Fire chief William Green said: 'We think it was a gas blast. It's a miracle that anyone got out alive. We will be considering a medal for Pascoe.'
> Tony Walsh, 30, said: 'It was a nightmare. The whole thing just went bang. It was an enormous explosion. We all owe our lives to fireman Pascoe who got us out. I really didn't think he was going to find Daniel. He deserves a medal. It was fantastic.'

Here is a suggested intro to get you started:

A couple and their young baby son owe their lives to a fireman who rescued them from their burning house in Carshalton early on Sunday morning.

5

General features

Why features?

Once you feel you have mastered the skills of news writing, you can then move on to what is arguably a more subtle form of journalism: feature writing. Most careers in journalism, however, are not so predictable and some writers are fortunate or unfortunate enough (depending on your outlook) to take up a position as a feature writer without ever having written a news story.

This is not as alarming as it sounds. Some writing styles are more suited to feature writing, such as a humorous style. It would obviously be a waste of time to employ a stand-up comedian to write an advice column on DIY problems in the home. It might make for entertaining reading, but the style or what is sometimes called the 'tone' of the article might not be right – to say nothing for the content. Some features require a serious approach; others patently do not. Half the job of the feature writer is choosing the right 'tone' for a particular subject.

It may seem odd to begin this chapter by looking at style, but writing features does allow a journalist to develop their own writing whereas writing news can do the opposite. For many journalists, then, it is often the urge to be more creative in their writing that will make them switch to feature writing after having served an 'apprenticeship' on news.

It is also the case that some freelance contributors to newspapers are not trained journalists but are specialists in a particular subject area. To this end, it is the writer's knowledge and experience of that subject that will interest the reader, rather than how the feature is actually written. In the case of a DIY column, it would make a lot more sense to employ a local painter and decorator to write the piece, than it would to commission Bob Monkhouse (unless of course Bob has just redecorated his front room in an interesting colour wash!).

Why do we need features in a newspaper? This is a question that has become more relevant over the past decade. With the ascendancy of other news media, such as radio and television, the newspaper, with its much more dated 'spin' on events, has found it increasingly difficult to provide something fresh. The rise of 24-hour news radio and TV has increased the pressure on newspapers to examine their role. Newspapers cannot be as immediate as either radio or television on important breaking news. This is not to say that newspapers have ceased to break stories; they still do so, but more and more through their features pages. These tend to be a new angle on an existing story rather than an exclusive news revelation. For example, there may be a running political story in which the paper commissions a notable politician in the debate, who has not previously commented, to write a feature or commentary setting out his position. This turns out to be a fresh angle on the story and is picked up by other papers, and radio and TV.

News can also become boring. Say this to a hardened news hack and you take your life in your own hands. But it is clear that news is, in most cases, a serious form and should be treated as such. However for the reader, and often the journalist, this can become a little tedious. By its very nature, news has to deal with facts, but both readers and journalists need new challenges and stimulation otherwise they will look elsewhere.

News is also objective. So, what is wrong with filling a publication with objective accounts of the latest increase in water rates? Nothing at all – but an opinion piece or sketch on such a potentially uninteresting subject could make the story itself a little more readable. News also tends to deal with subjects in a brief form. This has much to do with the structure of the news page, but in a tabloid newspaper it would be rare for a news story to run to more than 800 words. Turn to the features pages and you will see much longer stories, up to 1500 words.

A feature does not have to be lengthy though. Short pieces written for a column or a diary page are still, strictly speaking, feature stories. It is worth noting that all the words uttered on News At Ten would fit on a single broadsheet newspaper page.

Generally, the advantage of a feature is that it can deal with an issue or story in considerably more detail, and therefore it is able to tackle more complex subjects. As far as a story about water rates is concerned, a feature will be able to explain at length how the rates are calculated and what factors have led to an increase in prices. It will also be able to examine some of the deeper reasons, if any, behind the increases. In a news story, this sort of information can be conveyed only in a brief form. This does not make the feature superior; it merely demonstrates its completely different role in the newspaper. In the end, it is unlikely that the water rates story would even warrant a feature, unless the increase was spectacular.

Features are also very important to newspaper advertising. As a journalist this is only of passing concern, but the past 15 years have seen a growth in what is described as the service feature. This is a story that is often closely related to a consumer product or products, informing the reader about how such a product can, for example, improve their quality of life. It can be anything from sun-dried tomatoes to a stairlift. Essentially, these features are normally read by people with money to spend and this encourages advertisers to book space in the newspaper or magazine. If you want to read examples of this type of feature, simply look at the news-stand where consumer magazines now dominate. We live in the age of the consumer-orientated feature, in which even an interview with a soap star is driven by our consumption of such programmes on television.

So, we need features in newspapers because they are often everything that a news story is not. They can be more interesting, subjective, personalized, opinionated, lighter, humorous, more in-depth and more stylish. As we look at the feature in greater detail, these distinctions may blur a little, but essentially these are the qualities which go towards justifying their existence in a 'news' paper.

How do we define a feature?

The dictionary gives us a good lead. 'An item or article appearing regularly in a newspaper.' But that in itself is not sufficient because many articles are not used on a regular basis. However, a further entry says: 'A distinctive part or aspect of a landscape, building or book.' All we need to do is take out 'landscape, building or book', and replace it with 'issue, event or person' and we have a working definition: 'A feature story is an item or article in a newspaper or magazine that brings to light a distinctive part or aspect of an issue, person or event.' If only defining news was so simple.

Such a definition opens up the entire world to a feature writer, to say nothing for the way in which the feature is written. There is literally no subject that cannot be the subject of a feature, if it is well researched and written. In news, however, many subjects rule themselves out, simply because they do not bring anything new to our knowledge of the story. The joy of the feature is that we may know all the facts of a particular story, but a slightly different slant in a person's column, for instance, may reveal a side to the story that we had never previously thought about.

Indeed, a feature can be about anything: people, places, events, practically all human experience, even the animal kingdom has a look in. Here is a piece from Outside Edge, a regular column in *The Express*. This was written by TV presenter Kirsty Young.

> A selective conscience is a wonderful thing. In recent years catwalk shows have been dominated by all things reptilian, from snakeskin hot pants to alligator clutch bags.
>
> If it moves, designers have been happy to dispense with its innards and stitch in a zip, unless of course it's furry – in which case the wearer had better duck the paint-bombs from protesters as she runs to the Merc...
>
> At London Fashion Week British design duo Clements Ribeiro was the latest team to suffer at the hands of the selective conscience brigade.
>
> Models from a leading agency refused to wear outfits, edged in mink... What's strange is that they don't display the same compassion when it comes to ostriches, lizards or plain old cows.

In this feature Kirsty highlights an inconsistency in the attitude of those involved in the fashion industry. She seems to make a fair point. The remarkable thing about this piece is that, despite its rather short attention to detail, it can actually be classed as a feature. It is not news as the facts contained in the story are not new: we have heard that it is London Fashion Week and that the designers Clements Ribeiro were boycotted by models from a leading agency.

Indeed, if you were to write a news story it would say: 'Designers Clements Riberio have been boycotted, etc' but this is a feature and it is meant to take the story a little further or at least entertain us. And so it does by pointing out that while boycotting fur, models do not have the same attitude to other creatures, namely: 'ostriches, lizards or plain old cows'.

This final sentence is known as a 'pay-off line'. It is the conclusion to the argument and makes the point that the writer would like the reader to remember. All features have a pay-off line as a way of rounding off the story.

The Outside Edge story demonstrates that a feature, in its smallest possible form, need be 'about' very little at all, but it must give the reader something to think about. Kirsty Young could not merely have regurgitated the facts about London Fashion Week – it would have been old news. Instead, she has satisfied our definition by bringing to light a 'distinctive aspect' of the story, ie the supposed hypocrisy of this agency. It is not an earth-shattering piece by any means, but it does put a different 'spin' on a topical story.

What makes a good feature? While some features may seem to add little to our understanding of the world, they all do have a central idea that drives them. This is the most important rule of features: the story will fall down in the writing if the idea does not 'stand up' or it has been ill conceived. Even the most stylish writer cannot make a readable story out of a bad idea.

Types of features

When you can confidently decide that a story should be written as one type of feature rather than another, you are nine-tenths along the road to understanding them. As a journalist you will be faced with myriad ideas that you feel could make a story, but what sort of story? Is it a news story, a news feature or an opinion piece, like Outside Edge? Once you have decided on the 'right slot' for your story, it will become much easier to write, because each different type of feature demands its own approach, tone and style. You can only fully understand these types by reading newspapers and being confident you can, for instance, identify a news feature from an opinion piece. Here are some of the types that you will come across in your reading:

Backgrounder

This is a very straightforward type of feature and is often tied to a recent event. A journalist will be asked to write a backgrounder when he has perhaps written the original news story on a particular subject and fully understands all its permutations. As a story, it is especially helpful to inform the reader about other questions connected with a complex news issue. If you glance through the weekend papers you will notice that the backgrounder pops up quite often, not only because the editor would like to fill the pages, but because the Saturday and Sunday papers are an opportunity to give the reader more details of a story that may have been running all week. They could be summed up as The Story So Far (plus some other details on top). Backgrounders can be anything from 500 to 1000 words.

A good place to find a backgrounder is on the foreign news pages. Events happening abroad are covered during the week, but mostly in a relatively brief form. This is where the backgrounder comes into its own, informing the reader where the story fits in the sequence of events during the past ten years and why it is significant. It is particularly helpful, for example, in the stories about Northern Ireland or Israel, where a long-standing conflict has passed through many stages, many of which the reader has forgotten or didn't know about.

In many papers the backgrounder takes the form of a box or panel on the page because of the demands of space. It can often turn up in point form with bullets (these are actual 'blobs' which make up a list) and gives a potted version of events to the readers. This is no less complete in terms of facts, but denies the reader any analysis of events, which is important for a good understanding of a complex story.

News features

This sounds like a contradiction in terms and fundamentally it is. Here we are attempting to explain the differences between news and features and suddenly we have a 'news feature'. Essentially, a news feature is a more detailed news story with a fresh angle. Often, it is only the intro which departs from the form of a news story, but commonly these stories could run up to 1500 or 2000 words in a broadsheet newspaper. You will always find news features, mostly in weekend titles, screaming at you from the news sections or news review sections. They are really the preserve of the broadsheet as tabloids rarely make the distinction between a news feature and a feature. In a tabloid, it will simply be a more detailed news story.

In terms of writing style, the news feature is the least subjective or opinionated of all the feature types. It includes many more sources than the straight news story and deals with issues in considerable detail. A typical news feature may be an exclusive story in a weekend broadsheet dealing with a series of political revelations. Perhaps a journalist has interviewed a number of 'unidentified' civil servants who have made claims about incompetence in a government department. This could be written as a news feature, drawing on several sources with a relatively 'hard' intro (more on intros later), taking the reader straight into the story and, importantly, allowing readers to make up their minds about the story. Given the level of opinionated journalism in newspapers, this would be a rarity and a refreshing sight.

Profiles

These are the bread-and-butter features of the modern tabloid newspaper, serving up information and detail on celebrities. The most popular way to research such a profile is through the newspaper cuttings facility, hence the term 'cuttings job'. Paper cuttings are now becoming very much a thing of the past. Most cuttings jobs are now put together using electronic material retrieved from the library.

The other main type of profile is the face-to-face interview, which allows the journalist to get a much more rounded picture of the interviewee.

Opinion pieces

This is where the journalist and the newspaper get to have their say. The most obvious form of subjective journalism is the leader article under the masthead of the newspaper, usually towards the middle of the paper, that puts forward the paper's view on a particular subject.

Another type of opinion feature appears opposite the editorial page on the so-called 'op ed' pages in broadsheets. The features editor or the editor will commission a writer with a background in a certain subject to write a piece that generally supports the opinion of the paper, although it is increasingly popular to publish a contrary view. The favoured topic for these is politics, but cultural and social issues also surface regularly.

Personal columns

To many, this is the plum job in journalism. Not only does the journalist get to write about practically anything he or she likes, but the sought-after columnist can command an enormous salary. There are many different types of column, from gardening to politics, from cricket to country matters.

The celebrity columnist is a relatively recent development. This is where a journalist from another medium such as television makes the move to newspapers. Generally, the aim of the column is to get people talking about particular stories and create some controversy. By its very nature, the column is opinionated and, it is to be hoped, more stylishly written than other types of features. Gossip columns, such as the William Hickey page, come under this category, too.

Consumer or service features

This is the newspaper as an information or advice service. With the growth of middle-market journalism (ie readers with a higher disposal income) in the 1980s, some sections of newspapers have been transformed into fact sheets, informing readers of the latest products in gardening, the home, travel and on the high street.

The idea behind this type of feature is to support the consumer-based advertising that is carried by the paper. This is not to say the features do not have to hold their own in the newspaper, but they are chiefly part of the package to inform the reader about consumer items. Even property pages can be included under this banner, as buying a house can be the ultimate consumer purchase. To pass the test of the service feature, a writer simply needs to determine whether the story is connected with a product or not.

Reviews

This type of feature puts the reader in touch with culture. Think of any artistic form and a newspaper will review it. The aims of the review are to give the reader both information and opinion on a cultural happening and perhaps to inspire the reader to visit the event, such as an exhibition.

Exercise 1: Pick the feature type

Here are the intros to five features. Can you identify each type?

1. Bedroom tussles are second nature to Bill Clinton.

2. As we prepare to make contact with the flower-bed for the first time in ages we should remind ourselves of some of the problems of gardening which the glossy books don't tell you about.

3. Grab your lifejacket, rearrange the deck chairs – a 'Titanic' wave is on the way.

4. Jane Gleeson, the enduringly alluring actress, has a new man in her life.

5. Worst things first. The major fault with this film is the actor Daniel Bryson.

(See page 137 for answers)

How to find your style

To be a good feature writer you will need a good writing style, and to develop it you will need patience. Your individual writing style will shine through only when you are confident about the way in which you use language. Until then, you will be uncertain of which word or phrase to use. And do not be daunted by the word 'style'. For our purposes, it means the way you use language. It has little to do with genetics or a God-given talent handed to only a few very fortunate individuals.

Style is something that every journalist can develop in their writing by simply allowing their own personality to come through. Once you do this, writing will be much easier, but you must first understand some of the more fundamental components of language. Become the master of language and your ideas will flow on to the page; struggle for the right verb or adjective and you will find yourself inviting writer's block. In essence, confidence in your abilities and good English usage will produce a stylish piece of writing.

There are three main elements to writing style, which can be applied, in general terms, to features. The first is the use of vocabulary. Always try to think of different words, even though they may well explain the same thing or situation. So much of journalism is describing what you have seen, so try to find a new word or phrase that can better encapsulate what you are trying to say. Also, use words in different contexts. Many phrases are overworked and you can always liven up a feature if you can turn around a cliché or well-worn phrase into one that more appropriately explains your meaning.

Do not always use the same sentence construction in your stories. Try using an extra clause to add life to a sentence. In news, the essence is always to get as much information across to the reader as possible, but in features you have some artistic licence. This is not to say that you can saunter off with several subordinate clauses, but try to challenge the reader wherever you can. You may find that if you are dealing with a complex subject matter, that this will suit your purposes. Also, think about using imagery or metaphors to give your prose a lift, but avoid making your language too ornate, because readers will think it pretentious and become bored.

Tone is a very important factor in style. When you sit down to write your feature have a clear notion in your mind of your attitude to the story. Do you think the story is funny, sad, tragic, unbelievable? When you have made some decision start to write and this attitude will then determine the tone of your piece. If you think the story should be given a light touch, inject some humour, irony or wit. If it needs *gravitas*, make sure you keep the tone serious.

Writers will also develop their own individual tone as they gain more experience. This tone is sometimes called the writer's 'voice'. It only means that every time you write a story, the tone of what you say is very similar. In many ways, once you have hit upon this, you have developed your own style.

Unlike news, there is normally more time to rewrite feature stories. If you do have this luxury take advantage of it by reworking any sloppy sentences. Literally, turn each one around by transposing the subject and object to help you think of a new construction. This process will keep you thinking about what to say and provoke some more ideas. Rewrite, and then rewrite some more because there are few sentences that cannot be rewritten successfully – including this one. For example, 'There are few sentences that cannot be rewritten successfully, so rework and then rework some more.' The second version of this sentence is preferable because the 'passive' voice has been replaced by the 'active' voice.

Style to suit

One of the greatest 'style' challenges you will face is determining the right style for the right publication. One reason is that popular tabloid newspapers, such as the *The Daily Star*, *The Mirror* and *The Sun* seem to have developed a language of their own. The best way to determine the style of a newspaper is to think about the reader. What do they do, how do they speak, what are their interests? Answering these questions will help you to gain a picture of the 'average' reader. Table 1 will also help you assess newspaper style.

Table 1 *Newspaper styles*

Broadsheet	Tabloid	Local
Formal	Colloquial	Conversational
Objective	Campaigning	Parochial
Rational	Sensational	Dramatic
Ironic	Direct	Literal
Challenging	Reassuring	Comforting
Wit	Pun	Visual gag

Obviously, papers will not stick rigidly to such a table, but they do try to be consistent in their style so they don't alienate readers. The most important role of the sub-editor is to make sure that there is a continuity of style throughout the paper and from day to day.

Readers of a tabloid newspaper are not then faced with a 1000-word analysis of the future of the European Union written in the style of a Victorian essayist.

Here are some more general style points to help you while you're writing:

- Try to maintain a simple sentence construction and avoid being too convoluted. The less contrived the sentence, the more apparent the style.
- Look for contrasts, contradictions and inconsistencies in the language of the subject you are writing about. Use these in the way you construct sentences to make them more interesting;
- Write as if you were telling a story to a friend from the publication you are writing for. This is good way of drawing your instinctive style to the surface.
- Try not to be too clever. You are trying to communicate as effectively as you can, hopefully in the warmest possible way. By being too clever, your readers will sense a know-all and turn the page. Do not at any time talk down to or patronize the reader;
- Try to write about areas and subjects that interest you. By doing so, you are more likely to feel inspired as you write, and therefore more creative. If a subject leaves you cold, you will struggle to write stylishly.
- Do not copy someone else's style. This is very tempting, but it is a shortcut to nowhere as not only will you be found out but you will find writing far less rewarding. The fact is that there are no shortcuts to developing a style and you must be patient. Simply put: the more you write, the more your style will develop.

The structure of features

The structure of a feature story does not vary substantially from a news story. The obvious difference is the intro, which can be written in a far more imaginative way than in news. The most important departure from news is that the pyramid structure is turned upside down. The new inverted pyramid illustrates the theory that sometimes the background to a news story could actually be used to make the first line of a feature, depending on how it was written.

This does not mean that you should start a feature with a throw-away line, but it does demonstrate that you can attack a feature from many different angles.

As with a news story, each new point needs to be linked in some way to the previous one to maintain some sort of logical flow. It needs to be a rational arrangement of ideas, not just a series of observations – and it needs to have a conclusion of some sort. This is another distinct difference with news. Whereas a news piece can simply end on some pertinent fact, a feature needs a 'pay-off' line, in which the writer refers to the intro in some fashion. It can simply reiterate the thrust of the intro, but it is better for a pay-off line to take the point a step further. Tabloids have a habit of being prescriptive, almost recommending a course of action for those involved in the story. Here is the structure of a small gossip story from the William Hickey diary page in *The Express*. While these appear to be short news stories, diary pieces come under the umbrella of features.

> Times are hard at Planet 24, Bob Geldof's once-hip television company, as its flagship The Big Breakfast limps into ratings oblivion.
> Geldof's wunderkind partner Charlie Parsons, responsible for The Word and inflicting Terry Christian and Amanda de Cadenet on the nation, famously enjoys the trappings of his success. Now, I discover, he has been rendered chauffeurless.
> 'Charlie's chauffeur, Kit, is leaving today,' reports my man with a beard trimmer outside Geldof's office, 'and he is not going to be replaced because they want to save money.'
> Parsons, 38, who has come far since his days as a trainee reporter on the *Ealing Gazette*, will have to share a driver with fellow-director Waheed Ali and, on occasions, even drive himself. 'People are quite worried,' I am told, 'Charlie hasn't driven regularly for some time and he's not very good.' My sedan chair is available, but only in emergencies.'

The first point to note is the immediate similarity with news structure. The intro takes you straight into the story, saying that 'Times are hard at Planet 24', giving you a notion of what the story is about. Of course, it is not strictly speaking a news story, otherwise it would have said something like, 'Planet 24 director Charlie Parsons will no longer have a chauffeur because of cost cutting at the television company that created The Big Breakfast'. Written as news, the story seems reduced to the trivial.

But when it is written as a feature, a far more subtle start eases the reader into the story. It is also highly unlikely that this story would make the news pages – it simply isn't earth-shattering enough. The other substantial difference with a news story is the tone, which is a good deal lighter than my reworked intro above. And typical of a gossip column, it is light but slightly cutting. Note the sarcastic reference to Terry Christian and Amanda de Cadenet being 'inflicted on the nation'. No such column is complete without such a barb, a very popular technique with tabloids.

The story does not actually make its point until the end of the second paragraph, where Hickey says: 'Now, I discover, he has been rendered chauffeurless.' With a suitable pay-off line, the story could probably end here, but we then hear the evidence to support the revelation. It turns out that Hickey has spoken to a man 'with a beard trimmer' outside Planet 24, who not only gives us the chauffeur's name but, more importantly, why he has had to be replaced. Notice that, despite its status as a feature, the gossip column is still answering several of the news questions: *who, what, why?* The only difference is that there is no great compulsion for these to be included in the first or second paragraph. Indeed, it is the third paragraph before we discover the reason for the chauffeur's departure.

The fourth paragraph takes us into the background of the story. It gives you the age of Parsons, not entirely critical but useful, and where he began his career, which effectively demonstrates how successful he has been. It includes a little more detail on the story about how the car share will work and leads us towards the pay-off by setting up the fact that Charlie may not be the best driver in the world. Again, this is all sourced by the mysterious man outside Planet 24, who, we must assume, loiters there on a regular basis. The final line is a good quip about the offer of the use of Hickey's sedan chair, adding a sense of familiarity and warmth.

Exercise 2: Pay-off lines

Can you think of three alternative, funny pay off lines for the end of this feature? Each line should be one short sentence and make reference to cars or driving.

(See page 137 for answers)

Writing feature intros

The feature intro, sometimes described as the lead, has the same function as the news intro but there is greater freedom in how it can be written. Gone is the restriction to include the news facts, *who*, *what*, *where*, *when*, *why* and *how*, and less important is the emphasis on trying to grab the attention of the reader. The reason why the attention factor diminishes is that the reader is now bombarded by not only a headline but also (normally) a small 'standfirst' (introduction) or 'strapline' and a large picture. This combination draws the eye of the reader to the story as they make their way through the paper.

The feature also has less competition from other stories on a newspaper page. With a news story it can be placed at the bottom of the page where many readers may not necessarily look, let alone read. This is why the attention-grabbing properties of the news intro are paramount. With a feature intro we can afford to construct the lead in a more interesting and imaginative way, 'leading' the reader more gently into the story. This does not mean that you can start a story, 'Yesterday, I went to interview a very interesting man.' The glory of the feature lead though is that there might be an occasion when this could make an intro — if, for example, you wanted to highlight, with a degree of sarcasm, just how uninteresting the interviewee happened to be.

Look at the intro used in the above story in more detail:

Times are hard at Planet 24, Bob Geldof's once-hip television company, as its flagship The Big Breakfast limps into ratings oblivion.

Most stories in gossip columns are reasonably short in length so they need to be densely packed with information. This is also why their intros tend to resemble closely their news equivalents. The above intro certainly falls into this category, telling us fairly straightforwardly that 'Times are hard at Planet 24.' You could make no more obvious a statement of what is going on at Planet 24. There are many different ways of attacking this subject. Let us say that you were writing a much longer feature on the travails of Planet 24 but based on the same details.

You might wish to be a little less literal in the intro or attempt to make a joke by saying, 'Bob Geldof's once-hip television company, Planet 24, seems to be drifting into a new and more spartan galaxy'. In the alternative version, the idea is to write a lighter intro around the name of the company.

The second half of the intro still does not spell out the entire problem at Planet 24, but does usefully outline some of the background to the story. It points out that The Big Breakfast, one of the company's most popular offerings, continues to slip in the ratings. This is crucial as the reader can immediately identify with this programme and it also gives the company some status and a reason for appearing in a gossip column, other than the fact that Bob Geldof, eminently newsworthy in any situation, happens to be associated with it.

Mentioning The Big Breakfast and Bob Geldof in the intro gives the story a reason for being there, a topical reference point. The 'peg' or 'hook' as it is sometimes known, upon which you hang everything else in the story, does not come until much later, when it is revealed that a director has 'lost' his chauffeur. In fact these are the two essential ingredients that make a feature: a topical reference point and a 'peg'.

Notice that the intro makes no attempt to explain why The Big Breakfast continues to cause problems for Planet 24; this would be the subject of a quite different feature. In essence, this intro reflects the 'news' style of the column itself, rather than its status as a feature. It delivers the *who* and some of the *what*, but in a much jokier tone than, for example, a news feature.

In general terms, the length of an intro should be no more than 40 words. It should be up to three sentences long and normally take up one paragraph. These are not hard and fast rules but guidelines. Many tabloid feature intros are just a single sentence, whereas broadsheet leads are much longer. This has much to do with the detail and length of the story itself and does not indicate that one is better than the other. One of the most interesting exercises for a student journalist is to examine the way different papers attack the same story. It is difficult to say that one is right and the other is wrong, but it is definitely possible to say that one is 'better' than another.

There are several different types of feature intros. The 'news peg' intro, which is similar to the one analysed above, is one of the more popular styles. Simply put, it takes a news story as its peg and writes the intro around it. Here is a good example of the type written as a political feature in *The Express*:

> John Major has got used to saying that by-elections don't matter. He said it after the voters of leafy Newbury inflicted a massive and humiliating defeat on the Tories in 1993. He said it after the voters of Christchurch followed suit a few months later. He said it when the Tory candidate was catastrophically beaten out of sight at Eastleigh.

This intro encapsulates perfectly the story, despite being 60 words long. In fact, the first sentence tells you where the story is going: it is about John Major and his apparent dismissal of by-election results. It also makes you want to read on. It is a news peg intro because it uses the news story of the day – the Tory defeat in the Wirral by-election – and takes it further.

Another popular alternative is the 'narrative intro'. As the name suggests, the intro attempts to 'tell a story' in the crudest possible sense. The key to writing a good lead in this style is to think that you are starting to write the first sentence of a novel. This will concentrate your thoughts on 'what happened first to this specific character'. Try to pick out an incident in their life, preferably one that is related to the story, and recount it in detail.

The 'teaser' intro type tries to give the reader a taste of the story with a simple line that encourages them to read on. Roy Hattersley, as television critic at *The Express*, begins this review with a good teaser line, which couldn't help but make you read on:

> Flatby is a fishing town somewhere in England. It is inhabited by people who know absolutely nothing.

The glory of this intro is its simplicity and tone. It draws the reader immediately into the subject, but leaves you asking whether Flatby is real or imaginary and why the inhabitants are so ignorant. It turns out that the 'inhabitants' are fictional in a sitcom called The Perfect State and he goes on to criticize the characters as stereotypes.

In each intro you need to think through what is described as the 'feature angle'. Most intros tend to deal with the *who* fact and the *what* fact, but they also have that 'distinctive aspect' to the story that a reader will find interesting. In this sense, the feature angle can be a reinterpretation of the norm, the expected or the conventional.

For example, 'Flatby is a fishing town' is the norm, but that everyone there knows nothing goes beyond what we normally expect, even if they are fictitious.

When you come to writing your intro, first list the *who* fact, the *what* fact and then the feature angle. This will help you to analyse the information so you can draw out the most interesting details. It is unwise, however, actually to write your intro based on a certain type. Every feature will warrant a slightly different approach so do not attempt to write a narrative intro for each story; it will become too contrived.

The profile intro needs to encapsulate something interesting about the interviewee in one or two sentences. In many ways it needs to 'sell' the person in much the same way as an advertiser would. Here is the profile intro of actor Toby Stephens written for the *Sunday Express* magazine by Andrew Duncan.

> With the talent of his mother and the charm of his father how could he fail, but, he said, he was paranoid when asked to play *Coriolanus*. 'I thought there'd be jealousy and I'd end up with knives in my back.'

This intro shows the '*who*, *what*, feature angle' approach. The *who* is Toby Stephens, the *what* is Toby playing in *Coriolanus* and the feature angle is that despite his family background he was paranoid about playing the part. Note the simple construction of the opening as it leads you directly into the apparent contradiction faced by the actor.

Other types of intro include the quote intro, which self-evidently starts the story with a quote. This is particularly useful in a profile, where the interviewee has said something startling that seems to illustrate the story in a more striking fashion. It is worth remembering that 'breakout quotes' are sometimes used on the page itself to highlight a particularly good piece of the interview (or by the page designer as a typographical device to break up slabs of text).

There is the 'question intro', which seeks to raise the central issue of the feature with a query. It is good way to start a politics feature in which the writer is putting forward some argument as a point of debate. However, they can be used too often and become a lazy way of starting a feature. It is better to think of a conclusion before you start rather than try to develop one as you write the story.

Finally there is the 'ironic intro', which, as it indicates, sets up some sort of false proposition to draw the reader into the story. For example, 'The M6 is one of Britain's great motorways: it's traffic-free, hassle-free, blessed with services and today celebrates its 20th anniversary.' This is obviously untrue for anyone who has driven the motorway and thus readers will be intrigued as to why the story is so blatantly false.

Here are some other general points about feature intros to remember:

- Try to represent the idea behind the feature, not simply choose a style of intro and then begin writing.
- Tell the story as if you are telling a friend, and that includes the intro.
- You do not need to start with the most important fact, rather the least important in many cases.
- Look for a particular detail in the story, something slightly off-beat, quirky, tangential to begin with. Think laterally to 'find' an opening line.
- Just as with a news story, try to grab the attention of the reader and entice them to read more. Don't forget the story itself may run to 3,000 words.
- Every feature needs to have at least two good lines: one to start with, and another to end.
- Simple sentences are often the best.
- Don't forget: there may be a standfirst, strapline and picture as well as a headline to tell the reader what the story is about.

Exercise 3: Feature intros

Reread the story about Planet 24. Write four intros in four different styles: narrative, ironic, question and quote.

(See page 138 for answers)

6

Specialist features

Profiles

There is no doubt that there has been a considerable growth in the number of profiles published in daily papers, both tabloid and broadsheet. It is not only in newspapers where the growth has occurred. There are now several magazines, for example *Hello*, which are devoted exclusively to celebrity profiles and interviews. Of course, profiles can be written about people from any walk of life – even your next door neighbour – should he turn out to have the world's largest model train set tucked away in his back bedroom.

However, the main reason for profiles is to satisfy the public's appetite for gossip about famous people. It would seem that people are insatiable about every possible detail about a celebrity's life, from the style of socks they wear to what they keep in their freezer compartment. Along the way, the reader discovers how the 'name' achieved the climb to the top of their profession but, in many cases, these traditional biographical details are secondary to the more titillating and 'gossipy' information. Much of the reason for this is that the standard of celebrities being interviewed has shown a steady decline, so a great deal of the information revealed is bordering on the tedious. Of course, if you are sent to interview a so-called 'middleweight' celebrity it is your job to find something interesting and move away from the strictly titillating – if, indeed, you are allowed to do so by your editor.

There are other more positive motivations for interviewing personalities. The first is to try to find out something about the way that they think; this may seem a little irrelevant sometimes. One of the upsides to the cult of celebrity journalism is that the 'net' now drags in people who would once have been excluded, such as 'popular' scientists. This is where a virtue can be made of what is ostensibly a low-brow form of journalism by interviewing people who have something worthwhile to say. These considerations, of course, depend on the type of publication.

The main reason that tabloids often interview personalities or VIPs is to explore a private side of their lives. It is true that people often have a 'public face' or an image that is used for the media, but a more in-depth interview can uncover a side to their personality which has never been seen. When this happens, profile writing is at its most interesting and goes beyond the simple gossip style treatment. A good profile can also be inspirational, certainly aspirational. Many readers may look to some personalities as role models. Personalities, on the whole, are achievers and we can learn from them.

From a journalistic point of view, a profile also allows you to develop your writing in a different direction. It is a challenging feature to write and you sharpen both your interviewing and analytical skills. As a feature writer you may discover that most of your time is spent doing profiles of one sort or another, certainly if you work for a national newspaper. Profiles also carry a high level of reader loyalty and people will return to the same page each day or week to discover what a different celebrity has to say on a certain subject.

You may think that celebrities would detest the intrusion into their private lives. In general, the answer is yes, but most are aware that their livelihoods depend on a certain amount of publicity and, even if they are not particularly aware of this, their agents certainly are. This is certainly the case when it comes to profiling actors, especially Hollywood film stars, who are offered to the right sort of publication, from which the 'right sort of publicity' can be guaranteed. Hollywood film agents will also try to ensure that one particular set of pictures is published, rather than a set of images that may not be appropiate for the role the actor is playing in an upcoming film. It is also the case that most heavyweight film stars are simply not available for interview unless a movie is due for release. Because of this, do not expect to write a feature about 'Whatever happened to so and so?' as any potential bad publicity will not be welcomed. This situation is a little less manipulative in Britain, but publicity will always be geared to events, rather than the whim or idea of a journalist.

Profile types

The first type of profile feature is where a particular celebrity is interviewed for their opinion on a story of the day. This can be because they work in a related field or they are an expert on the subject. When journalists want a quote on how prime ministers treat their press secretaries they invariably turn to Sir Bernard Ingham, Lady Thatcher's former press secretary. Such a quote can often become a short profile to illustrate a point in more detail.

Another style of profile is the big face-to-face interview, which deals comprehensively with someone's life because of a recent event that has thrown them into the news. This type of feature is the staple of the Sunday colour supplement.

Some 'ordinary' people are often profiled because of an unusual aspect to their lives. The *Express on Sunday* once ran a series of articles called My Weekend, in which people were interviewed because their weekend pastime was an unusual contrast to their working life. It was a great success. Someone can also be profiled for having the best collection of pencil sharpeners, though this is far more likely to occur in regular feature slots like collecting.

The authoritative profile is common in the weekend broadsheets. As with the face-to-face interview, it is an attempt to give the definitive summary of the life of a person connected to the story of the week. It can be very opinionated and reasonably selective about the type of background that is included, to support a certain view about the person. The writer will also interview people who know the subject of the profile, so the story has real depth.

One of the most straightforward profiles you will read in the newspaper is the obituary. This is an attempt to provide a very balanced account of someone's life, often written by someone who was close to the dead person. When you look over an obituary page it may appear to you that many of those written about do not strike you immediately as being very famous. The reason is that the obituary page, as well as covering the death of many personalities, also aims to write about people who have had interesting lives. In this respect, it is the story of their life itself, rather than any celebrity status, that is the reason for the obituary.

One of the great growth areas in this type of feature has been the 'celebrity vehicle' or 'special focus profile'. In many ways these are contrived vehicles for bringing celebrities to the reader, and are often structured as a first-person interview in which the same questions are put to a different personality each week. This type of feature has become very popular in the Sunday colour magazines, which pride themselves on discovering new 'vehicles' for introducing celebrities. The *Express on Sunday's* one-time *Boulevard* magazine was entirely devoted to such features.

Here are some examples of this type of profile: Relative Values; How we Met; Life in the Day; At Home; My Favourite Room; Shall we Dance; My Favourite Photograph. In the *Express on Saturday* magazine, there is also a feature that examines the contents of a celebrity's fridge.

How to structure a profile

As with all features, the intro is quite important, though not critical. It is worth remembering that most profiles will include a picture and a standfirst on the page, so you can afford to attack the lead in a slightly less direct way. This is an example of an intro for actress Juliette Lewis, in *The Express*:

> When Brad Pitt got engaged to Gwyneth Paltrow last year, headlines screamed that he had broken the hearts of women everywhere. But one woman was really devastated. 'I still haven't got over him. I probably never will,' admits actress Juliette Lewis, even though she and Pitt split in 1994. 'I'm resigned to the fact that I'll always be in love with Brad.'

This is a long but thorough intro to the story, supported by a headline 'Why I'll always love Brad', a picture of Lewis, and Lewis and Pitt, plus a standfirst, saying 'When Brad Pitt left Juliette Lewis, she tells Jane Dowle, she turned to drugs then God.'

The angle of the story is how Lewis has been devastated by the departure of Pitt from her life. This is reinforced by the so-called page furniture (headline, standfirst, etc), so the intro needs to attack the subject at a tangent. In the end, it opts to start the story where the trauma actually began: when Pitt got engaged. Using narrative intro style, it takes you immediately back to last year, when the story broke about the engagement, 'setting up' the heartbreak for Lewis.

The intro then includes what is perhaps the best quote of the piece 'I still haven't got over him. I probably never will.' The writer could actually have begun the story with this quote; it is strong enough. The 'hook' for the profile, you may be surprised to learn, is not the Brad Pitt break-up but a film due for release the following month called *The Evening Star*. This does not get a mention until the fifth-to-last paragraph, and probably doesn't deserve a place any earlier. While it does seem that she has only been made available for interview because of the release of the film, the profile would lack an angle if it simply began with the line: 'Juliette Lewis is set to star in a new film next month: *The Evening Star*.' It is far more 'newsworthy' to discuss her relationship with Brad Pitt because he is a far bigger star.

The intro ends with a quote that backs up the headline: 'I'm resigned to the fact that I'll always be in love with Brad.' This neatly wraps up the intro, making it self-contained. While none of the details of the relationship has been outlined, we do read the two most important quotes. The test – even for a features intro – is does the intro stand on its own without the rest of the story? In this case, it does. Don't forget that many readers flip through a newspaper, sometimes only glancing at the headline and the intro before moving on. As with news stories, it is just as important in features to write self-contained intros. Not only does it set up the story well, it provides a good précis of the feature.

Unlike many Hollywood 'puffs' of stars before their latest films, this profile attempts to cover the serious issues surrounding the break-up of her relationship. In a later quote it reveals the consequences of the break-up:

> I drove on the wrong side of the road with a car coming straight at me. And I was smoking a lot of pot back then. It made me totally anti-social, unproductive and intolerant of people, and that's such a waste. I really hate the stuff now.

When it comes to the general structure of a profile, use as many quotes as possible. This may not be possible in many profile types, such as the straight cuttings job, but in a face-to-face interview they are crucial to the structure. The quotes used need not be verbatim but they should carry the essence of what has been said. You can even include snatches of conversation you may have had with the person before or after the interview to give the story a relaxed feel and a context. It also demonstrates to the reader that you were actually in the celebrity's home, rather than just trawling through a collection of cuttings. It is said that a good interview is one-third cuttings, one-third quotes and one-third the writer's observations. These proportions can vary, but offer a good rule of thumb.

You may also want to include quotes from other sources about the subject of the piece. These may support or counterpoint your opinion, but they should not simply be used to support a particular view of your own that the subject has refused to agree with.

Inject as much descriptive colour as you can. Not necessarily the fabric type on the sofa or the colour of the coffee mugs, but certainly what the person was wearing and a brief description of what they have inside the house. If it is a face-to-face, the reader will want a description of the celebrity's appearance, how they speak and their demeanour throughout the interview. If you are doing the profile over the telephone, it is still possible to make an observation about their manner – whether the person was very forthcoming, for instance.

Background is a very important part of a profile. The reader needs to know all the significant moments in this person's life. Of course, many would take too much explanation, but a potted version in most instances (ie a couple of paragraphs) will suffice. If the person outlines their past in a quote all the better – use it.

Make a decision before you start writing on the tone of the profile. All good features of this type tend to take a position about the subject of the profile. This does not mean that you set out deliberately to destroy someone, but your attitude will shine through in your copy so why not make a conscious decision before you start on whether you should be deadly serious or slightly flip. If it is a profile with an actor or actress, the tone can be a little lighter than it might be for a politician, though the latter may produce their own comic moments.

Don't forget that many 'stars' will have copy approval, which means that you will have to fax your completed story to the agent concerned. Some newspapers have a policy against copy approval, which is a positive development. Copy approval seems to defeat the whole purpose of journalism because readers look to newspapers for a lead, not for anodyne publicity stories.

Some newspapers also agree to interviews, offering not 'copy approval' but 'sight of copy prior to publication', to check for factual accuracy.

The cuttings job

This type of profile should only be used as a last-resort measure, such as a late-night obituary. Here you assemble background for your story about a personality from a series of cuttings which are printed from a computer-based newspaper cuttings library. Essentially, it is a fast way of gathering information about someone in the news.

The cuttings job, however, is a pale imitation of the face-to-face interview. Its only virtue is the speed with which a profile can be put together. The modern cuttings system can deliver you a hundred or so cuttings on a celebrity after a five minute session of research on a computer, whereas an interview may take hours to source.

Beware of inaccuracies in cuttings. Try to find at least two stories that reveal the same fact about someone, rather than relying on just one source. There is nothing worse than a paper repeating the same mistake, or even adding to it. If the person is famous, you may also be in danger of repeating a libel, so try to steer away from less reliable publications or check with an on-duty lawyer.

You may also fall foul of copyright law, which applies to all published material. As a general rule, you are permitted to use information from a published story which is already in the 'public domain'. This includes such banal things as a person's age, where they live or where they went to school. All these 'facts' are considered to be in the public domain. However, more detailed information or particular claims about a person, which you then repeat, could land you in trouble. Three factors will govern any breach of copyright: the amount you copy, the nature of it and other information that you add to the story. There is no rule of thumb about how much information can be 'safely' copied from another story, but there is a 'fair dealing' defence, which applies to stories that are in the public interest or reviews. In both instances, however, you must attribute the source, ie the other newspaper.

Copyright is an important issue, and newspapers have been known to sue over exclusive stories which have been 'lifted' by rivals. With all researched material from other newspapers and magazines, it is wise to use only background information rather than actual quotes or any unsubstantiated claims.

Face-to-face interviews

Many journalists find this a far more rewarding way to put together a profile. It allows you the luxury of time not only to interview the person concerned, but to think about how you should approach the story. And it will show – it is a far more thorough way to discover something 'new' about the subject. You may come to some new conclusion about the person by reading the cuttings, but it will not reveal anything that hasn't been written previously.

Essential equipment for the face-to-face interview is a small tape recorder or Dictaphone of some sort. It is the most reliable way to record a conversation, which ostensibly this is, or at least should be. You will need a notebook as well to jot down the odd point, but it is better to maintain eye contact with your interviewee throughout. It shows that you have nothing to hide, even if you do, and that you are not merely scribbling down your shopping list for the evening supermarket run.

The important part of the interview happens before you leave the office – research. The interview's success will depend on what you know about your subject. Why conduct the interview, you may ask? The aim of the interview is to get a far more rounded picture of the person, rather than the potted version which filters through the cuttings. You are hoping that the interview itself will throw up something new, and it often does. Use the cuttings to swot up on your interviewee. Make sure you know everything that can be known about them before you leave the office. Also look in *Who's Who* and other reference books so you are certain about the person's age, for instance, and any family that they may have. Colleagues can also be helpful in this situation. Take a note of people's by-lines on the cuttings and, if you have time, chat to them about who you plan to interview. There may be a 'Don't mention the war' question, in which case, ask it! But not at the beginning of the interview – or it may end abruptly.

You may also find it worthwhile to interview acquaintances and/or colleagues known by your interviewee. Often they can reveal information that would rarely turn up in cuttings. They may also suggest whole areas of questioning that you had not considered. Take a full note for the record of these conversations because they may be worth using in the final story.

Prepare at least ten questions for the interview around a theme or angle that you have decided upon. Some journalists would say that this isn't necessary but planning an approach is never a wasted exercise. If it transpires that the interview turns up something completely different then go with your instincts, but your 'planned approach' can still be used when writing up the story. The questions should be a combination of direct questions (When did you start collecting bus tickets?), leading questions, ('They can be quite interesting, bus tickets, can't they?') and open-ended queries ('What do you like about bus tickets?'). In general, have more questions than you need, as you will be surprised how quickly some of them are answered.

During the interview itself, make an effort not to rush the process. Of course, all of this will depend on their schedule, but if there is time, use it. If you have the option of deciding where the interview will take place, go to the venue of their choice, preferably their home. This is not only so you can be nosy (within reason of course), but also the interviewee will be more at ease there. Also, if you have a photographer or 'snapper' with you, let them do their business first. This acts as a good ice-breaker and most people tend to relax a little while having their photograph taken. If they don't, you can expect a tough time.

It is also worth remembering that people are increasingly wary of journalists and believe most to be insensitive, uncaring beasts with the lowest of all motivations for being involved in the press. Try not to live up to the stereotype and turn on the charm and politeness. Being aloof and arrogant will get you nowhere.

Try not to talk too much – a contradictory piece of advice for interviewing you might think. Although it may not be obvious from the start of an interview, the whole exercise is about *them*, not you. Small talk is obviously important, but during the actual interview there is probably nothing more boring for the interviewee than to have a journalist spouting their own views.

Try not to appear a know-all. Again, this can be a major 'turn-off' for an interviewee. If you follow every answer with an 'Oh, yes, didn't someone else say that recently?', you will quickly find that they have lost interest. In short, appear interested. Try to keep your conversation to questions alone, rather than engaging in private debate. Of course, this will depend on the subject. If, for instance, you are tackling an alleged corrupt councillor over fraud claims, you shouldn't be too polite. The 'bottom line', however, in interviewing is that the subject can always order you from the building or put the telephone down, should you be doing the interview from the office.

Make an effort to understand every response you get before moving on. Do not simply agree with the answer if you have absolutely no idea what they mean. Probe a little: 'What do you mean by that?', 'Why?', even 'I don't quite understand'. Often these are the moments that produce a story as you are forced to dig a little deeper to discover some clarity.

Embarrassing questions

Do not be afraid to ask the embarrassing questions. In a sense, interviewees expect them, although they wouldn't be disappointed, I expect, if you didn't ask them. People's private lives are always difficult to tackle, so do not sail headlong into this subject without first prefacing it with, perhaps: 'Do you mind if I ask you about your girlfriend/husband, children?' With a celebrity interview, however, the ground rules may have already been decided with an agent. On the more delicate subjects, give the interviewee time to answer; don't rush them. You will often find that a silent pause, here or there, will allow them to become more forthcoming. When an interviewee feels comfortable in your presence, the more revealing they will be. Also, it helps for you to spend as long as possible with them, so the interviewee can properly relax and trust you.

Frame your questions with the key *who, what, where, when, why* facts because these will get you a response that is not confined to a simple 'Yes' or 'No'. These so-called 'news facts' will help you sort out the story in your mind as you prepare for the interview. If you have no time beforehand, try to be conscious of starting each question with one of these words. It also conditions you to ask questions, rather than merely make statements to which the interviewee can either agree or disagree.

Think of the questions that your readers would like answered, because it is not your view alone that counts. If, for instance, you happen to be interviewing a genetic scientist for a tabloid newspaper try not to immerse yourself too deeply in the theoretical side of the subject, but rather issues of a more practical nature that readers will find interesting and relevant to their lives. Do not deliberately 'dumb down' the entire process, however. Readers will be alienated if you patronize them with too simplistic a version of the story. It is up to you to find the balance between the two. Obviously, if you are doing the story for the *New Scientist*, readers will have a genuine interest in the scientific detail, not so with *The Sport*.

Try to avoid asking trivial questions. This may seem like the most important thing to uncover in a feature, ie more detail, but it is better to have researched it beforehand. For instance, don't be tempted to ask a well known film star how many movies they have made. While they may have the answer ready to go, the question does smack a little of a lack of preparation. Before you leave the office, check out such details with an agent, PRs, reference books and cuttings. It is also better not to expose to the interviewee your ignorance. Not only do you appear ill informed, but you also show that you have little interest in what they've done. Even if you are interviewing a politician it is far better to come across as something of a 'supporter', rather than a long-standing critic. People do like to feel that they have done something worthwhile, hence the justification for doing a profile in the first place.

Colour

An interesting way to break up a string of quotes in a profile is to write descriptive colour. This is not an invitation to launch into a narrative about every piece of furniture in the house, but it does give the reader a feel for the way the interviewee lives. When the interview takes place in an office, this type of description can also be used. The objects on a person's desk – at one time the subject of a feature in itself in the late *Boulevard* magazine – can be very revealing.

Another good way of interrupting a seamless run of quotes is to write about the way the interviewee answers questions. This often reveals as much about the person as the answer itself, so beware of irony and humour. Always, strive to convey to the reader how you *felt* about the person you interviewed, how they came across to you. If you feel that the person is aloof or detached, do not be afraid to say so. You might begin a sentence: 'Aloof and detached, the actor Ben Carter is a different prospect off-screen, than on'.

All of this is of interest to the readers because you are a cipher through which they can try to understand this person. This attitude does encourage a subjective approach to interviewing and profile writing and it will prove more interesting to the reader.

When you have finished asking the questions you have prepared, ask the interviewee if there is anything further they would like to add, or whether they would like to clarify an earlier answer. Such a query often brings a strange silence, but in some cases they may be eager to talk about a subject new to you. At this stage of the process it is inadvisable to make any deals about when the article will appear in the newspaper or how it may be written. Also avoid giving copy approval to the interviewee. Although difficult to bypass with some agents, insist that this was not agreed before the interview was granted, if this is the case. As a last resort, point to the fact that copy approval is against the policy of the newspaper, which it is likely to be in any case.

You may ask, what is wrong with giving copy approval? On the face of it, it does seem like an innocent request. The real problem lies with interviewees who are abnormally sensitive to public criticism, the numbers of which seem to be growing by the day. Fundamentally, the profile interview is a subjective process by a journalist attempting to outline the character and motivations of another person. It is not a piece of publicity or so-called 'puff'. In these days of spin doctors and minders, journalists need to be increasingly aware of the dangers of allowing 'outsiders' to control what appears in the newspaper. Most publications are reasonably

independent and this seems worth preserving. If you can only publish something that is positive about someone, it may be better not
to publish at all. It seems like a dishonest exercise in the extreme.
Far better not to bother because readers will become suspicious of
too flattering a critique of anybody.

It would seem that there are obvious exceptions to this rule,
especially if you happen to be breaking a big news story. Your
source may say that he would not like a certain incident in their past
mentioned, which is irrelevant to this particular story. If the story is
important and is in the public interest, I would not hesitate to agree
which such a condition. Judge each request against the importance
of the story, as in many cases the interviewee needs the story more
than the publication does.

At the end of the interview ask if you may telephone at a later
stage to clarify any points. It is likely that during the sub-editing
process other journalists may wish to check certain details.

Writing the story

How much information will you need to write your story? A good
rule of thumb is that an hour's interview will make five, typed A4
pages or about 4,500 words. Ample, you might say. The problem is
that much of what you have recorded will be unusable. It will make
for interesting background, but it will often not give a good selection of quotes.

Despite this, it is wise to make a transcript of the entire interview, as it is much easier to edit from a written page than it is from
a tape. If you have time, type out the entire interview (you can now
buy software that does it for you from a recorded interview) on to
your computer, then print it off. The best way to deal with the raw
material is to mark the points in the transcript that you find interesting, and strike through the remainder. Once you have done this,
it becomes a simple assembly job, arranging the quotes into a formal structure.

Don't forget you will need to have thought about an angle for
your intro at this point. This will be an aspect of the information you
have gathered that you feel reveals something new about the interviewee, something that you have not come across before. If you've

not looked through the cuttings at this stage, do so – it will give you inspiration.

One of the best ways to choose an angle for your piece is to recall the interview itself. Ask yourself: was there any one answer that made you listen more intently than all the others? Invariably, there will be – and that will be your angle. It may even be the simplest, throw-away line in your interview.

If the feature you are writing is 2000 words long try to go for a punchy, off-beat intro. The reason is that much of the 'hook' for the story will be covered in the standfirst, headline and captions. If the reader digests the first two before starting your story, then the intro will need to start on a different tack.

This is why it is often better to remember the image of the inverted pyramid, where the least important quote now takes its place at the top of the story. So look through the transcript for any throw-away lines that refer obliquely to the general subject of the interview. Do not try to construct an elaborate intro; it simply isn't necessary. The best way to think of the intro is that it is your job to tantalize or tease the reader. After they have read this, their imagination should be stirred enough to make them want to read on. Do not put your best quote at the beginning of the copy; in the top third certainly, but not at the head of the story.

Imagine yourself reading the copy for the first time, literally as you are writing it. Continually ask yourself: Is this passage necessary? Am I getting bored at this point? Is there a better way of writing this? How can I liven up this section? Can I rewrite this quote slightly to make it more interesting? As we have discussed in the news writing, you do have some leeway in reworking quotes, as long as you do not completely alter the sense of a passage. One experienced profile writer from a national newspaper once said that he always rewrote quotes; he said it was the only way he could make some people interesting!

This sort of policy is best avoided, but it is worth saying that the quotes you have gathered will not always make for good English. The interview is a conversation, so it is likely that your interviewee will speak in short phrases and unfinished sentences, in which case they will need to be remoulded and put in some context. Remember: all the copy should be readable, not just your pieces of narrative in between the quotes.

About half of your copy should be in direct speech. Do not be tempted to write more narrative than is necessary to carry you from one quote to the next. Your job is to link one passage to another and allow the copy to flow logically, to tell its own story. In that sense your impressions of the interviewee are secondary to any opinions that you may write into the feature. If you have a particular view of the person, you should allow them to respond to it during the interview itself, rather than introduce it during the copy.

As with other features, make sure you have a good pay-off line that reiterates the main point of the feature in a conclusive way. This is your opportunity to make your opinion known but not without some foundation. In other words, any view must be supported by the quotes, otherwise it is simple editorializing.

Exercise 1: Face-to-face questions

You have been offered a face-to-face interview with Mick Jagger of the Rolling Stones. List ten questions that you might ask him on the fortieth anniversary of the Rolling Stones' first gig.

(See page 138 for possible answers)

Reviews

Writing a review is one of the most opinionated tasks that a journalist can be asked to do. Unlike many other types of feature, a review (also known as a critique or notice) is an opportunity for you to say exactly what you think. It will need to be in the style of the newspaper of course, but here you have free rein to say anything you like about that Oasis gig, that Chris O'Donnell film, that Martin Amis book, that EastEnders episode.

Reviews are not exactly a growth area, but they have a place in almost every newspaper. Specialist sections have now appeared in many weekend papers, which are devoted entirely to reviewing the week's cultural happenings. For example, the *Sunday Times'* Books section is widely read and respected by all those who have an interest in literature. Reviews come in less rarefied forms in tabloids, where the coverage and the detail are considerably less.

Fundamentally though, reviews give information to the reader on a cultural activity. They will tell you what the show, book, etc, is and who is involved with it. It will also give you an opinion of the work by someone who has expertise and authority in this field.

The review is also a form of advertising and this should not be taken lightly. A good or bad notice can thrust a work into the limelight. In this respect there is no such thing as bad publicity. The notice is also a form of public record. *The London Theatre Record* keeps a cutting of every professional play that is reviewed in London.

Another purpose served by the review is to provide entertaining copy for the reader. A story about the previous night's episode of EastEnders, given the reservoir of knowledge about the programme, can make for interesting copy. Also, you will often find that literary editors will ask novelists and writers to review the works of their fellow artists rather than give the task to a staff journalist. This can produce a review that is far more interesting and readable than the book itself. In this sense, a good review is a piece of journalism in its own right and not just a publicity handout. A review can often be kept by readers as a souvenir. People collect all manner of things concerned with the arts, and this will include reviews of particular art forms in which they are interested.

Writing a review

What should you include in your review? The first and most important facts are those about the people involved in the work. Make sure these are spelled correctly and that you have clearly defined each person's role, not confusing actors with directors, painters with gallery owners and authors with editors or publicists. If necessary, find out some background information on those concerned *before* you do the review as this will help you put the work in context.

You will need direct quotes from the film, book, show, etc, to support any points that you are making. Do not simply criticize a work without using some evidence to back your opinion. Some of the better critics can simply say they didn't like something and, of course, they are perfectly within their rights to do so. But a review is strengthened if the writer can support his view with a quote from the play, for instance, which demonstrates that a particular character was not very well drawn and unrealistic.

Do not give away the ending. This is a common fault among reviewers who fail to understand that many people may wish to attend themselves. Readers will get very upset if you spoil their entertainment for them. Not only is it a review, but also a preview.

Explain the plot or idea behind the work in simple language, even if you're reviewing a play about chaos theory. Do not pitch your review at the same intellectual level as the work of art, since your main task is to interpret the work for the reader, not test them with it – ie if you can solve this, you can go to the play. Reduce the piece to its main elements (in a play: acting, set, story) and attempt to explain all of them. Another way of approaching the review is to deal with why the work has been created in the first place. This will give you a good starting point, then you can judge whether you think it would be suitable for your readers.

It is always good practice to be a little sensitive towards those you are reviewing. If you find yourself about to review an amateur dramatics group, think twice about what is achieved by being too critical. Try to look for something positive in everything you see as it will give your review balance. If you use every notice to slam everything you see or read, you will lose the attention of the reader, who will simply conclude that there's no satisfying you.

Libel

Try not to libel anyone as it can be very costly. There are several key points to remember, but these are the boundaries used by a court in deciding whether you have damaged someone's reputation:

- Does it lower the plaintiff in the estimation of society?
- Does it bring them into hatred, ridicule, contempt or dislike?
- Does it tend to make them shunned or avoided by society?

It is up to you to decide whether a piece of criticism is fair comment, but fundamentally there needs to be ample evidence for the claim in the work itself. Obviously, if you are malicious in any way, you will fall foul of the lawyer, who is employed by each national newspaper to read all the pages before they go to press. Here is an example of a piece of fiction copy that goes a little too far:

> Peter Randall's performance of Dan, a wife beater, couldn't have been more realistic given his own troubled domestic life.

This notice couldn't be more libellous if it tried, amounting to a straightforward accusation that the actor is a wife beater – without any evidence whatsoever that this practice is going on. It is not good enough to praise the actor for a realistic performance, while at the same time making an unsubstantiated allegation.

The best way to avoid a libel is not to be too hostile. Of course, it could be argued that a good review needs to be honest, but you should err on the side of the caution when you criticize personalities associated with a cultural happening. A far better way to approach a very critical review is to target the show or exhibition itself, rather than individuals involved. This is often difficult to avoid, but in this way you highlight a failure on behalf of a group of people rather than a soon-to-be embittered artist.

A review must have structure – just as other features should. It must also have an angle or idea behind the intro. It cannot just exist because the play or otherwise has been put on; it must stand on its own as a proper feature. Take Roy Hattersley's intro, which we discussed in the last chapter.

> Flatby is a fishing town somewhere in England. It is inhabited by people who know absolutely nothing.

There is obviously a new sitcom which Mr Hattersley, as TV critic, is obliged to write about. However, he doesn't begin the review by stating simply that a new series began the night before on the BBC. He begins by 'teasing' the reader about the residents of fictional Flatby, who, he says, know absolutely nothing. This may seem like fair comment to most of us, but this rude tone will encourage you to read on, especially as you don't know whether the town actually exists.

Another reason why the intro to a review must be outstanding is that in a section specially devoted to notices it is likely that your review will be competing with others. Readers of these pages will run their eye across all the headlines and intros before they settle on something that they would like to read. When you are pondering over your intro, try to think of a sentence that encapsulates the idea behind the work of art. This has two purposes: capturing the reader's attention and giving them a sense of what it is about.

Think of your intro as a way of selling the show to the public as a copywriter or publicist might go about their work. Of course, if you found the entertainment wanting this may be a little difficult, but again you are trying to 'sell' your idea to the reader – to make them read on.

Try to write strictly to the length set by your editor. This does not matter so much with other features, but a review, which might be filed as late copy for news pages, will need to fill a specific hole in a page. It may therefore be hurriedly subbed or restructured, in which case your finely crafted argument may end up on the cutting-room floor. If it is 300 words, write no more than 320 and learn to 'sub' your own work.

Write for your readership. If you are doing a review for a tabloid newspaper about a Samuel Beckett play on the West End, do not suddenly lapse into discourse on existential philosophy. It is not that many of your readers will not understand such a point, but it will be inconsistent with the rest of the newspaper. Tabloids tend to concentrate on the personalities, the actors involved in the production, the drama and any sex. On the other hand, broadsheets will normally focus on ideas, arguments and maybe the work's cultural impact.

The tone of the review will also be completely different. In a tabloid it will be mocking, damning or praising, while the broadsheet tone will be more analytical, less effusive and more measured generally. Try to aim your review at the type of audience that you think would be interested in the subject matter. This tends to be a little hit and miss, but bear in mind that a performance of Puccini at the Royal Opera House is likely to attract a different patron from a new series of Gladiators on ITV. Cultural boundaries do blur, so take care.

Leader articles

This is your opportunity to be as opinionated as you like, and not be criticized for it, in fact praised. Leader articles or editorials appear under a small masthead of the newspaper towards the middle of the newspaper. They do, however, get dragged to the front of the newspaper if the editor considers that a story is important enough. This normally happens at an election or moments of national tragedy or disaster. Generally, though, the leader is a wide column of copy with a single, small headline and no picture.

The purpose of the leader is to express the opinion of the newspaper through a news story. This opinion is always the editor's – though the writing might be done by any number of senior people. It could be subtitled the 'something to be done column' as it harks back to an age when newspapers felt that they could substantially influence public opinion and the public decision making processes. It could be argued that papers still exert some influence on the political agenda, but this would seem to be waning. Even *The Daily Telegraph*, which has been described as the 'conscience of the Conservative Party', cannot claim to hold the sway over politicians that it once did.

So, why are leader articles now necessary? The first reason is that they emphasize the newspapers' role as an editorial form as opposed to simply a vehicle for informing the reader of the 'news' of the day. So many other media, such as radio and television, provide an 'objective' framework for the news agenda without acknowledging their capability for shaping opinion. In this sense, newspapers have traditionally provided a 'lead' and they are unique in this role.

Second, leaders also seek to explain complex issues. It is another opportunity for the paper to describe exactly how a particular issue affects the reader and why it is important. Third, an editorial should provoke debate. In many respects, a newspaper is a forum for debate and a leader helps to initiate and sustain this. Recently, newspapers have increased the space for readers' letters as a way of involving more people in discussion over issues. Newspaper readers have opinions and it is the paper's duty to provide them with a platform.

Last, an editorial tends to make an issue more important in the reader's mind – give it more authority. By its very nature, it tells the reader that perhaps they should take a second look at this particular question and consider it in detail.

So why does an editorial carry more authority than an ordinary feature? This is a matter of debate, but basically the leader is printed without a by-line, expressing the opinion of the newspaper as a whole. A feature, however, is printed with a by-line and might not necessarily be the view of the newspaper, but rather a polemic aimed at stimulating debate.

The tone of the leader article differs substantially from anything else in the newspaper. The reason is that it needs to convey opinion rather than a series of facts as in a news story, or even a feature. The theory is that the reader will have already cast an eye over a news story and possibly a feature related to the subject before turning to the editorial. It would be unusual for the reader to turn initially to the leader, though the positioning of a leader on the front page tries to encourage the reader to do just this before reading anything else.

For the broadsheet, the tone is serious, analytical, instructive and prescriptive, often setting out a course of action for a politician or an organization. For the tabloid, the leader will be moralistic, assertive, even funny, but often with a stern underlying message. The idea is that you should read an editorial and change your views according to the way it is written.

One tabloid newspaper, which has had a notorious reputation for the use of its editorial, is *The Sun*, particularly at election time. One of its most famous pronouncements came in 1992, when its front page screamed:

> IF KINNOCK WINS TODAY, WILL THE LAST PERSON TO LEAVE BRITAIN PLEASE TURN OUT THE LIGHTS.

The inside copy said:

> We don't want to influence you in your final judgement on who will be Prime Minister. But if it's a bald bloke with wispy red hair and two Ks in his surname, we'll see you at the airport. Goodnight and thank you for everything.

This is an example of a tabloid leader using humour to put across a very serious point: ie that you should not vote for Neil Kinnock. It is remarkably direct in its treatment of the subject – another tabloid trademark. In this sense, they are written more in the style of a picture caption than an editorial. If you are called on to write such a leader, you should not mince words but tell the reader how to think or behave.

How to write a leader

You will need to research an editorial like any other feature, gathering information from different sources to support the view you will take. Make sure you have a clear sense of what you are trying to say. Do not be tempted to start writing and, as you do, make up your mind in the process. Give the reader a strong indication from the beginning that you know your own mind.

Do not waver in what you are going to say, but put it with conviction. After all, we can assume that the reason that most readers are looking at this column is to reflect on the view of the newspaper. Before you start, make a list of the reasons which support the position you are going to take. This logical process will help you arrive at a sensible conclusion. If you have been told a view to take, do this in reverse order, ie conclusion, then your list of reasons. As you will discover, there is an argument to support almost every point of view.

Offer a lead to the reader, hence the term 'leader'. If you don't feel strongly about an issue, find someone else to do it – if you have a choice in the matter. While you are effectively 'telling a reader what to think', avoid being patronizing. Do not talk down to them, but rather challenge them with your strong views on this particular subject.

The most important line in an editorial is the last one. This is the punch line, the conclusion, the sentence that will recommend some course of action or approach. In this respect, it is as much like a traditional essay as anything you will come across in a newspaper, offering, as it does, a conclusion to a problem. In fact, most editorials are the answer to a problem, eg how you should vote in the General Election.

Leaders should be written very tightly. Just because you are expressing an opinion, this is no excuse for over-writing. Try to put your case in short, simply constructed sentences, which clearly state the view of the paper. Don't forget that some tabloid editorials may be only three sentences in length, so you will need to get to the point very quickly.

Do not be concerned that you may be put in the position of having to write an editorial about a view that you don't wholeheartedly support. It is often the case that some journalists on a particular paper will not support the stand taken by their editor. This is not as alarming as it sounds: you are a professional journalist and there are many shades of opinion. However, do not be afraid to argue your corner, if you are fundamentally against a particular opinion expressed by the paper. It may be possible to use this as a counter-point somewhere else in the publication.

Personal columns

As mentioned in the last chapter, writing a column is viewed as the plum job on any newspaper, not least because of the large salary often on offer. The column provides the journalist with nearly unlimited scope to say what he actually thinks about a certain subject. It is also a step up from the leader because, in the column, you can put an opinion that may not necessarily be the view of the paper at all.

What is the purpose of a column? The reason that there are more and more columnists in papers is that they sell papers. A good national newspaper columnist will carry readership from one paper to another, boosting circulation as he does. An example of such a writer is Anne Robinson who is a columnist for *The Express*, having previously written for *The Mirror*. It is easy to see why editors view columnists as such an important part of the newspaper.

Columnists also add personality to the newspaper. In recent times there has been a drift of celebrity writers from television to newspapers, which has helped to raise the profile of the papers concerned. Again these personalities will bring with them loyal supporters who will then, it is hoped, read the rest of the newspaper. The paper also becomes identified with the celebrity, in many ways representing the 'type' of reader that the paper is targeting. Much of this strategy seems to be built around marketing, rather than the ability of certain columnists to be able to write an entertaining piece of journalism.

However, it is certainly true that columnists build up a strong personal following, reinforced by a picture by-line. Particular writers can also be relied upon to support the same views, and this again adds to reader loyalty. This is not as easy to achieve with leader columns or feature articles, where a particular viewpoint may be more difficult to pin down.

Good columnists also amuse and entertain readers. It is much easier to inject personality into a column than it is with a feature, hence the scope for more stylish writing. A witty and thoughtful columnist will always attract readers.

There is also a special role for the columnists in the local and regional press. Here, editors rely on them to provoke debate over issues and in turn influence opinion. In smaller communities, a good columnist provides a public face for the newspaper, encouraging readers to buy the paper for the column alone.

What makes readers turn to a column? This is one piece of journalism that can often be described as a victory of style over content. Many columnists concentrate on domestic matters in their life, rather than topical issues. When this happens the tone and style of the writing is all important, since much of the subject matter is very mundane.

When you are writing a column the tone can be conversational, witty, ironic, subversive, irreverent, moralizing, authoritative, bitchy – but not necessarily all at once. The main aim is for your personality to shine through in the copy so the reader can relate to you as something other than another hack. Readers must feel that they have entered into a relationship with you – as either a friend or an enemy. People may dislike Norman Tebbitt, who has written for the *Sun*, but this is no reason not to read his column.

As with other features, you must strike the right tone for the newspaper. Do not artificially construct a tone or style because this is something you will have to develop over time. It may be years before you are offered a column, but there is nothing wrong with submitting ideas for one or even putting together a few 'dummy' pieces of copy to bring out your own style.

What do you write about? Anything, is the short answer. Columns continue to embrace a wide range of subject matter, which is one of their most endearing qualities. The most popular area for writers is topical issues, such as the news story of the day. This may be the latest political happening, where the columnist chooses to highlight a particular detail and make a wry comment about it. The more strident will use this as a platform to express their views or have a thorough rant – depending on the publication. There are several Fleet Street columnists who choose to do the latter and have a great following as a result.

The second most popular subject area is the domestic environment. A school of writers now scribbles away about what is happening to them in the home, a sort of 'What happened after breakfast'. Of course, this is injected with humour and style, but essentially it is a column in which readers can relate to the writer's circumstances at home. This type of column can be very funny, but also extremely dull if the writer does not lift it beyond the mundane. It is all very well for you to write about putting the cat out but, for it to be interesting to someone else, the story must be told in an engaging way.

Cultural issues also find their way into columns, especially in the arts and review sections. These often take the form of notebooks or diaries, in which the writer gives you a few wry thoughts from the past week. Again the emphasis is on whimsy rather than biting critique, providing the reader with a counterbalance to the many reviews in the section.

Finally, personal lives and relationships form a large part of the columnists' subject matter. This is where the writer involves you, literally, with the problems that beset their lives, including the extremes such as divorce and death. Here the reasoning is that readers will relate directly to the experience of the writer, rather than the personality of the writer themselves. This type of column tends to be of an occasional nature.

Here is an example of a lead piece from a column Outside Edge written by the actor Tony Booth in *The Express* – well before the 1997 General Election.

Lying in bed, stricken with the lurgy, I read the newspapers – and I am still puzzled by how the hell this Government gets away with it.

There was Agricultural Minister Douglas Hogg crowing that the Government's win in the beef crisis meant he could keep his salary.

Thank God for that! I've got nothing against Hogg the Younger personally but he does seem to think that charisma comes through talking through your hat.

I once had dealings with Hogg the Elder, now known as Lord Hailsham. I took to turning up at his pre-election meetings to ask questions.

On one occasion, a bevy of Tory three-piece suited heavies pounced on me and bounced me out of the hall.

The lengths these Hoggs will go to, to avoid answering questions. Looking at the present Cabinet, you can see that some things haven't changed.

The first thing to notice about this column is how the beaming face of Tony Booth draws you into the page. Why Tony Booth? The first reason is that he is Tony Blair's father-in-law and, in the run-up to the General Election, he may be able to give a special insight into how the campaign is unfolding. Second, he is a recognizable face from the TV sitcom Till Death Us Do Part in which he played a character with a very political outlook on life.

Here he chooses a reasonably serious issue to write about, but deals with it in a fairly light-hearted way. He begins by telling us that he languishes in bed 'stricken with the lurgy'. He immediately makes a political point so you are left in no doubt which side he will be supporting in the election, saying he doesn't know 'how the hell this Government gets away with it'.

His target is Douglas Hogg, the then Agricultural Minister 'crowing' about his efforts in the beef crisis. Tony Booth finally leads us to the point of story, which is his recollection of attending pre-election Tory meetings to 'ask questions'. He tells of being 'pounced on' and 'bounced' out of the hall. His pay-off line strikes a parallel between the previous and present Hogg and their respective abilities to answer questions.

One of the first things to note is how extraordinarily different the intro in a column is to an ordinary feature. It begins very slowly, as many columns do, assuming the reader is probably prepared to indulge the writer a little. There is no simple, teaser line to draw in the reader here. Imagine beginning a news story by pointing out that you are suffering from a cold, while reporting on a life sentence being handed down in the Old Bailey. It simply wouldn't be interesting for the reader, but in the case of a celebrity columnist it is. Why? The reason is that it creates a mental image of Tony Booth 'lying in bed' flipping through the newspaper before getting fed up with Douglas Hogg. Given the nature of his railing character in the TV sitcom, it is an image that springs readily to mind.

Another interesting aspect is the way language is used to lighten the tone of the column. First, there is 'stricken with the lurgy', a turn of phrase for being ill, a minister called Hogg 'crowing', 'talking through your hat' – a reference to Hogg's famous hat and finally 'pounced' and 'bounced' out of the hall – a well-executed rhyme. All of these serve to give the column some texture and style and lift it from the ordinary. It is fair to say that Tony Booth has quite a lively style in his own right, putting aside any reputation he may have as a TV actor or the relative of a well-known politician.

In terms of subject matter he seems to combine three typical areas. He uses a personal situation as his starting point, ie in bed ill, adds a topical reference about the travails of Douglas Hogg and finally works in a recollection of his past political activities. The all-important pay-off line draws effectively the three lines of attack together, saying that the tactics of the Tory party have not changed from one Hogg to the next.

7

Other forms of journalism

Production journalism

Roles in production journalism, such as sub-editing, are often seen as the poor relation to a career in feature writing. And while it is true that there is certainly less glamour attached to proofreading than interviewing a pop star, production can have its own rewards. Many sub-editors enjoy the challenge of writing headlines, captions, 'polishing' the copy and bringing stories to their final proof stage before printing.

The role of the sub

This differs from newspaper to newspaper, but essentially the sub-editor takes the first step towards putting the actual paper together. Along with the editor, the chief sub-editor will discuss where a particular story should be placed on a page, which picture should be chosen to illustrate it and how the copy should read. Once the copy arrives on the subs' bench from the reporter, it is the job of the chief sub to read it through for sense to make sure that it meets the requirements that were discussed earlier with the editor or head of department.

If, for instance, some copy has been filed on an aspect of a flood disaster, such as the rescue operation, and the copy relates only to the building of sand banks in a completely different location, it would obviously have to be rewritten. The sub's role then is to look at the content of the newspaper logically, deciding whether a story fits the brief and how it relates to the rest of the page.

In many cases, however, it falls to the sub-editor to make the copy work. This is because it is often too late to rewrite the copy substantially or have new copy filed. This may involve rewriting the copy so that it relates to the picture chosen or suggesting a way of cutting it that would make it more suitable for the page.

Checking

This is the first and most important duty of the sub-editor. Each story will have a number of names that will be need to be double-checked. These will include names of people, locations, books, films and businesses. There are three ways that a check can be carried out.

The first is to consult a reference book. These will be held either in the library at the newspaper or in the department if it is a specialist department such as business or politics. This way of checking can be a little time consuming so it is always best to keep a few volumes handy for quick reference, such as a dictionary and a gazetteer or atlas. The former can be used for most of the basic checks and larger dictionaries carry a good range of biographical information.

The second way is to check the reference on a newspaper cuttings machine or in the library. This gives every reference to the person, place or thing that has been mentioned in a newspaper story. Choose an authoritative publication, and do not rely, for instance, on the *Daily Sport* to give a conclusive spelling.

The final alternative is to talk to the writer of the copy. Many argue that it is the responsibility of the reporter to make sure that the spellings in the story are correct. This is so, but it is also true that it is the job of the sub-editor to make sure that every word in their 'subbed' version is correct. If it is a word that is new to you, it is best to make the writer your first port of call as he may well have noted the correct spelling of such an unusual word. If this is the case, you can be reasonably assured that you have the right spelling, though a second, quick check can never go astray.

If all else fails you will be forced to rely upon your own judgement. Many sub-editors keep a list of unusual words or an editor's dictionary at their desk. The thoroughness of the checking will always depend on the time available, as most sub-editors will be working close to the deadline, so bear that in mind when you troop off to the library for a half-hour clarification of a spelling in middle English. The last resort in these circumstances is to fall back on the subs' mantra: 'When in doubt leave it out'.

Grammar

This is the second key duty of the sub-editor: to render the copy into plain English. The approach to style and English usage will differ from publication to publication, but as a rule you should ensure that all copy has sentences that are simply constructed and easy to read. The basic laws of grammar apply, but there is less need to become pedantic about such things as split infinitives. Readability and sense are the bywords, so don't get too bogged down with grammatical rules which may indeed be lost on many readers.

Rewriting

There are two schools of thought about sub-editors rewriting copy. The first, and most traditional, is that the sub-editor's role is to perform a straightforward proofreading task and write a headline and caption. The second, and more radical view, is that the copy you receive from the writer is simply the first draft, which can be used as the basis to write a much better story that is perhaps more consistent with the style of the newspaper. This view is more prevalent in tabloid newspapers, where the style of writing and tone of the paper seem more obvious than a broadsheet. It is also the case in many features departments, where outside contributors are used and the style of the copy is variable.

The best approach to take on rewriting is pragmatic. If you feel a piece of copy is not consistent with the style of the paper, makes little sense in places and is lacking a proper structure, suggest to the editor or head of the department that it be rewritten and outline how best to do it.

Do not, however, set out to rewrite copy just so that you may do some writing yourself. Usually a chief sub will tell you if a rewrite is needed. The job of the sub-editor is not to gain a by-line by the backdoor because, in most cases, the original by-line will stay and your hard work will have been in vain. Your job is to make the copy more readable so that the ideas put forward by the writer are communicated more effectively to the reader.

Again, time will be the guiding factor. Often in news there is little time to rewrite long passages, so confine yourself to making sure that the intro is as sharp as possible and does justice to the story. If it does not, write a new one that includes the key who, what, where, when, why facts.

Headlines and captions

In the eyes of many, this is the most important task of the sub-editor. There is no mystery to headline writing as some sub-editors would have you believe. Equally, it is not simply a case of reading a story and thinking of the first thing that pops into your head.

When you read the copy, try to think of key words related to the subject. The sub-editor should become a walking thesaurus, able to think of new words to describe the same action or the same object. The best headlines are active, containing a verb and telling a story in themselves. Do not simply repeat what you find in the copy because the sub-editor should avoid repetition wherever possible.

Try to match the tone of the story. If the copy is a serious piece about a refugee crisis, do not leap in with a comic headline that includes some lame pun. Alternatively, your gravest headline should not be put forward for a tongue-in-cheek feature about yuppies going into sheep farming in Yorkshire. Choose your target carefully and your headline will hit the mark.

When trying to write a headline about a feature, it is often helpful to think of clichés and common phrases that can be reworked in a humorous way. Pick out a single word from the phrase and try to think of a word related to the story that may rhyme with it. This type of headline is the staple of newspapers and will always draw a reader's attention to the story – the reason we have headlines in the first place.

Do not try to be too clever. In news headlines, your job is to interest the reader in the story, not the headline itself. It is not the job of the sub-editor to write a headline that is more cryptic than the story. The reader should be drawn to the story by key words in the headlines, rather than puzzled by what the story might be about.

For captions, the same technique and approach apply. Think of a line that best explains the picture and do not forget to mention all the people in the photograph, unless it happens to be a football crowd.

Photojournalism

This is a specialist area of journalism that can appeal both to trained journalists and photographers alike. It contains all the best elements of journalism but works with a different raw material – images. Instead of words to describe a story, the photojournalist will submit a set of pictures.

Photojournalists cover all sorts of stories, but most have made their reputations photographing wars, famines and other large-scale stories where their graphic images have captured a moment of suffering or joy that even the most descriptive copy couldn't rival. This is why photojournalism still has a place despite competition from television, because a single picture can convey an enormous amount of detail and emotion.

Many photo stories submitted to newspapers and magazines are done in black and white, rather than in colour. The reason this type of picture can tell a story more effectively is that it does not have the distraction of colour. While the British press does not publish a great deal of photojournalism, there are a few notable exceptions, including some Sunday supplements such as the *Express on Sunday* magazine, *Guardian Weekend* magazine and *The Independent* magazine, the last of which was a pioneer in this area when first launched.

The biggest market for photo essays of this kind is the Continent, especially in France and Italy, where picture editors, who buy the photo sets, have a greater respect for pictures than their British counterparts. So, if you're aiming to sell a sparkling photo essay, your first port of call should be *Paris Match* rather than a British national newspaper.

How do you get started?

One of the best ways to learn the trade is to join a regional newspaper after your training. This course of action is a good way of getting a grounding in the business. Here you will learn about what makes a newsworthy picture – a journalistic skill that can only be

picked up on the job. You will also learn about the latest technological advances in news photography, in which it is now possible,
with digital cameras, to transmit images from your car to the newspaper page in 40 minutes.

So, how do you succeed in this very competitive market?
Unfortunately it is not simply a case of rushing around with your
camera snapping what you believe to be a newsworthy event. To
become a good photojournalist you will need not only the skills of a
trained journalist but also the technical abilities of the photographer,
which include understanding light, lenses and film.

When you are considering a career in photojournalism you must
think carefully about the sort of photography that you wish to do.
Depending on your point of view, photojournalists do not have the
most enviable working life, dashing from one job to the next at locations around the globe. This may affect your personal life, coupled
with the fact that the financial rewards are not great or immediate,
unless you happen to establish a very good reputation and can command large fees for your pictures.

The best way to establish yourself as a photojournalist, after a
suitable training course, is to become a member of an agency. These
are companies, often set up by photographers, which distribute pictures around the world to papers and magazines. They take a cut of
between 20 and 30 per cent, depending on the photographer or
agency. If you happen to be with an agency, it will handle the distri-
bution of your photographs as well as commission you to cover certain stories. With an agency, you maintain a certain amount of control of the pictures.

The alternative is to act as a freelance, leaving you free to travel
to Bosnia, for instance, where you will take a set of pictures then sell
them directly to a newspaper or magazine. In this circumstance, the
publication will buy your pictures outright, which is called 'all
rights', then syndicate them to whom they choose. The advantage of
the second avenue is greater freedom, while the attraction of the
agency is that they will help you with your expenses if they decide
to despatch you to Bosnia.

If a constant life of globetrotting does not sound particularly
attractive, there are alternatives. You might consider feature photography, which includes fashion, food, still-life and beauty. This is
undoubtedly a growing market, especially when you consider the

wealth of weekend newspaper supplements and consumer magazines on the news-stand.

Most newspapers and women's magazines include a fashion feature of some sort and the advantage of this type of photography is that it can sometimes be done in a studio. This means that you can establish a base rather than transport equipment, including lights, from one location to the next. Food, still-life and beauty photography are also predominantly studio based.

Photographer Annie Leibowitz, who is renowned for her celebrity portraits, uses a crew of 20, such is the amount of technical equipment required to take outstanding pictures. This type of photography also requires the 'snapper' to establish some rapport with the subject of the photo shoot. If you do not, you will end up with a set of pictures that lack warmth and fail to bring out the best in the person you are photographing.

Another form of 'celebrity' photography, which is not so glamorous and is constantly the target of criticism, is paparazzi photography. Here, the financial rewards can be great and immediate. But if you become a member of the paparazzi your life will not be your own. These snappers literally camp outside doorways and houses for nights on end, hoping for that elusive shot of a celebrity. Often the celebrities they are pursuing have already left by a rear exit. The 'pack' are most notorious for following members of the Royal Family and pop stars.

To be one of the paparazzi you need to be tenacious, tough and ruthless, but above all have a dream that one day you will scoop the world with that special photograph. Do not be fooled into thinking that this has anything to do with photojournalism as most paparazzi pictures don't even attempt to tell you a story. This is the world of the opportunist. You simply aim to capture a moment, which says, for instance, that Noel Gallagher of Oasis has just bought a T-shirt from a high street store. You may also find yourself in breach of the PCC Code of Practice if you infringe someone's privacy. The market in Britain for such photographs is expected to contract after Princess Diana's death, with newspapers sensitive to the public's wish not to publish intrusive photographs.

While you may be attracted to news or feature photography, you should not limit yourself to one particular field. As an aspiring photographer you should try to gain skills in several different areas, such as food or fashion, to develop a style of your own. This will allow you to support any forays into photojournalism with the more obviously lucrative areas of photography. In the end, photojournalism can be a hard slog, in which you can go to great expense to pursue a story but finally fail to see your work published.

You must learn the technical skills as well as the creative ones, for example lighting. Many people who concentrate solely on photo-journalism predominantly done outdoors would struggle to light a studio properly for a food shoot. Photojournalism is also not for the faint hearted. You must be physically fit and be able to lug around a large bag containing a couple of cameras and lenses. It is also a career that seems to divide along gender lines. It is difficult to say whether it is simply the 'gung-ho' nature of some photojournalism that proves a deterrent, but few women seem to be attracted to the life.

Training

The industry recruits a small number of trainee photographers each year. You will need five GCSE passes at grade A–C, of which one pass should be in English. The minimum requirement to take the one-year full-time course at Stradbroke Centre is one A-level plus four GCSE passes or equivalent. Alternatively, if you have less than the above qualifications, but have had at least two years' experience of photo-graphic techniques, you will also be eligible. In many companies you will be eligible for a National or Scottish Vocational Qualification after undertaking a successful period of work experience. Stradbroke Centre is part of Sheffield College, Spinkhill Drive, Sheffield, South Yorkshire S13 8FD; 0114 260 26000.

8

Getting started

Roles in newspaper journalism

Journalists fill many different roles on a newspaper, which vary little between local papers and national titles. The following are the most common positions to be filled on a newspaper.

Reporter

With the virtual demise of the copyboy in the newsroom (the boy who took the paper copy from one desk to the next), the reporter has become the most junior person in the office, excepting the messenger. It is their job to gather news over the telephone or outside the office and then write up the copy into a news story. Reporters also have a responsibility to generate ideas for stories.

Researcher/writer

This is the most junior position in a features department. Essentially it is a 'go fetch' position in which many small research tasks are carried out, from the spelling of someone's name to the range and brands of deodorant used at a Battersea bus depot. Researchers/writers will also have small writing assignments to carry out, of perhaps 200 or 300 words.

Sub-editor

The most junior production position, the sub-editor reads and checks copy submitted by reporters and feature writers, looking out for grammar, spelling and sense. The sub-editor also writes headlines, captions and introductions, also known as standfirsts.

News editor

One of the senior roles in a newspaper, the news editor must set the agenda for the newsdesk each day. He initiates news stories as well as rewriting copy filed by news reporters.

Features editor

This is a senior features role, in which the features editor oversees the output of feature stories. Again, it is a dual role of developing ideas and dealing with copy from contributors and staff writers.

Chief sub-editor

A pivotal job on the newspaper, the chief sub brings together the copy submitted from editors and farms it out to sub-editors. He also acts as a revise sub-editor, checking over work carried out by the subs, and plays a part in the designing of pages.

Night editor

This is a key role overseeing the production of the paper from the subbing of pages to the design of particular stories. The night editor also has executive responsibilities over the production department.

Picture editor

This job involves calling in pictures for use in the newspaper and editing images. The picture editor deals with photographers and picture researchers; the latter's job is to track down particular images from picture agencies and libraries.

Art editor

An increasingly important role, the art editor designs the newspaper, setting the style for typefaces, headlines and the way pictures are used. The subbing staff will 'sketch' how a page should look, but the art editor, together with designers, 'draws' the page on the computer system.

Managing editor

An executive position, the managing editor is responsible for how the newspaper is staffed, who is employed there and how to pay for everything.

Editor

Usually the most senior editorial position on the newspaper, the editor has both managerial and creative responsibilities. He looks after the overall direction of the newspaper, its style, its tone and its political outlook. The editor's job is to provide a lead to the staff.

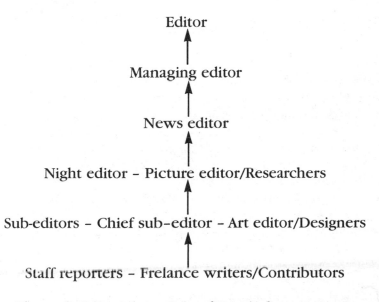

Editor

↑

Managing editor

↑

News editor

↑

Night editor – Picture editor/Researchers

↑

Sub-editors – Chief sub-editor – Art editor/Designers

↑

Staff reporters – Frelance writers/Contributors

Figure 2 *Editorial structure of a typical newspaper*

The editorial structure of a paper is a strict hierarchy (Figure 2), but may differ from newspaper to newspaper. Fundamentally, all stories and decisions are approved on one level before they can move to the next. In a sense it is a very old-fashioned structure, but it maintains control over the flow of work.

There has been little real change to the overall editorial structure of newspapers since they came into existence. To the outsider, it is a very undemocratic system and, while conferences are held at the various levels to discuss individual stories, power is vested in a few senior executives who guide the direction of the paper. Alternative structures have been suggested, such as one American idea in which journalists would take control of stories at each stage of production, from the initiation of the idea, the research and writing, through to page proof, but this has received little support.

There are also moves to change the role of the sub-editors. With advances in technology, sub-editors will become fully fledged editors with control over the production of an entire page rather than single stories. They will also have a greater say in the design of the page.

Training to be a journalist

Unlike medicine or the law, journalism does not have a qualification which is a standard throughout the industry. In this respect, it is more like a trade than a profession, and you will be hired because of your experience, education and any by-lines that you may have accumulated on perhaps a school or college newspaper. It is difficult to say how many jobs in newspapers are available in any one year, but it is estimated that in a good year there will be around 800 new entrants, and 400 in a bad one.

What qualities are newspaper editors looking for? You must be able to demonstrate a knowledge in current affairs at all levels, a lively interest in people, places and events, an ability to write in a style that is easy to understand, good spelling, punctuation and grammar, an understanding of what part local newspapers play in the community and a willingness to accept irregular hours.

Who does the hiring? Most jobs are to be found in the local or regional press, though some national newspapers, such as *The Express* offer posts for graduate trainees (details later in the chapter). However, the traditional route for an aspiring journalist is to start on a local title under the terms of a training contract or what is known as a *modern apprenticeship*. Forty per cent of journalists start this way. Both of these come under the heading of *direct entry*, which means that you have secured employment with a newspaper that runs its own training programme.

Direct entrants

As a direct entrant you will have a six-month probationary period, after which the newspaper will register you with the National Council for the Training of Journalists (NCTJ), a registered charity, and give you a distance learning pack of 16 units. The final unit is a test so that you can go forward to a 12-week period of college-based education and training, called a block-release course, during which you will have the opportunity to prove that you have reached a level of competence to obtain a National (Scottish) Vocational Qualification (NVQ) at level 4 or equivalent.

NVQs, which replaced apprenticeships, were introduced to the newspaper industry in the early 1990s and, while received with enthusiasm, many papers have been slow to take up the opportunity, some believing that there is too much 'red tape' involved. NVQs are obtained by demonstrating workplace competence across all the skills which go to make a rounded journalist. These skills are shown as units, each representing a specific task, such as generating story ideas or interviewing. An assessor decides when the requirement for each unit has been met. Units are collected, and when you have completed them all, you get your NVQ certification in newspaper journalism. The assessors are mostly editors.

Modern apprenticeships

There is an alternative form of direct entry, which enables you, as an employee of a participating company, to undertake relevant training leading to an NVQ level 4 in newspaper journalism: writing, news and features or in press photography.

Increasing numbers of publishers are taking in this scheme with the Training and Enterprise Councils (TECs). You will need to be aged between 16 and 23 years (graduates included), but you should have completed the programme by your twenty-fifth birthday. When applying for direct entry, you should ask the newspaper if they participate in the scheme.

Entry requirements

The usual entry requirements for newspaper journalism is a minimum of five GCSE passes (grades A–C) or equivalent. However, in recent years it has become rare for a trainee to be employed at this level. Over half the recruits into newspapers are university graduates, while many of the others have at least two A-levels. One of the passes at A-level or GCSE must be in English. A minimum of two A-levels or equivalent is often required for entry on to a full-time course.

Pre-entry

This means that you have undertaken an approved training course before obtaining employment. Once you are with a newspaper, you will serve a three-month probationary period before entering a training contract. As with the direct entrants, you will still be expected to prove your competence after a period of work experience. About half of all trainees recruited by the newspaper industry have attended a one-year, full-time training course for post A-level students and graduates.

There are a good range of training courses in print journalism that are accredited by the NCTJ. This body approves courses on the basis of a 50-point check-list, which includes 100 wpm shorthand, law for journalists, language, public administration (local and central government) and practical journalism, such as reporting techniques. There are also similar courses that are accredited by the National Union of Journalists (NUJ) and the Periodicals Training Council (PTC).

Graduate route: media studies courses

The number of graduates employed as journalists is growing by the year. If you decide to go to university, the best idea is to apply for a degree course in journalism, or should you graduate in another subject, such as English, you could consider a practical-based MA in journalism, which is now offered by several institutions. But beware of many of the graduate courses in media studies, which will not in fact train you to be a journalist and are much more theoretical in nature. According to NCTJ chief executive Rob Selwood, students who wish to train as journalists should be very wary of such courses because they will not provide you with a proper journalism qualification. The obvious exceptions are those degrees courses specifically in journalism, such as a BA Hons in journalism, accredited by the NCTJ.

This is not to say that media studies courses should be ruled out altogether. Research carried out by the Standing Conference in Cultural, Communication and Media Studies in Higher Education found that media studies students had a slightly better chance of finding work than other graduates. And there is no doubting their popularity. According to UCAS, more sixth formers now apply for courses in media studies than in mathematics, physics, chemistry or engineering.

There are literally hundreds of media studies courses offered by various colleges, which can lead to a Higher National Diploma (HND), a degree or a postgraduate degree, such as an MA. These can be found in the British Film Institute's book *Media Courses* (see below). The *UCAS Official Guide to University and College Entrance* also provides a listing, which can be found in your careers office or by telephoning UCAS on 01242 222444.

How to get a training place

The most popular route for the aspiring journalist is to become a trainee on a local or regional newspaper. Apply direct to the editor of a regional or local newspaper for employment as a trainee. The names and addresses of regional and local newspapers can be found in editions of various guides and directories, such as *Benn's UK Media Directory* (Miller Freeman Information Services) or *Willing's Press Guide* (Reed Information Services), both of which can be located in the reference section of your local library.

Two other publications which you could consider buying are *The Writer's & Artist's Yearbook* (A & C Black) or *The Writer's Handbook* (Macmillan). Both of these editions have a comprehensive listing of local, regional and national newspapers. Before sending your letter, compile a small portfolio of stories that you may have written for a school or college newspaper. You might also consider doing work experience at a local or national newspaper to see if you would actually like being journalist. During your attachment, you may get the chance to write a story, which you could then send with your application. In short, the more evidence that an editor has of your determination to become a journalist, the more likely he is to shortlist you for an interview. Do not be afraid to write to dozens of local newspapers as you will increase your chances of a place.

If you decide to opt for a full-time course before trying to seek a place as a trainee, apply direct to the National Council for the Training of Journalists (address is listed below), enclosing a 9 inch by 4 inch stamped-addressed envelope. Suitable applicants will be required to take a written test and then attend an interview. The tests are normally completed by February each year and the interviews will be conducted by Easter.

Paying for your course

If you opt for pre-entry, you will need to fund your own training. Local education authorities may award grants to meet all or part of the cost, but, because of the limited funds available, you will need to investigate this as early as you can. The authority will wish to know the status of the course, ie its accreditation, before it can make a decision. You might also investigate a career development loan.

Salaries

Regional (graduate) trainees often earn as little as £8700 for the first six months (possibly less for non-graduates), rising to £10,000 after attending a training course. Once qualified, you can expect to earn about £12,000. When you finally make the grade on a national paper, you can expect to earn up to £40,000 as a reporter, with the starting level around £28,000. The salary for sub-editors is similar.

NCTJ accredited courses and part-accredited colleges

Bell College of Technology, Almada Street, Hamilton, Lanarkshire
ML3 OJB; 01698 283100
Two-year HND

Bournemouth University, Dorset House, Talbot Campus, Fern Barrow, Poole, Dorset BH12 5BB; 01202 524111
BA Hons Journalism

Brighton College of Technology, Pelham Street, Brighton, East Sussex
BN1 4FA; 01273 667788
Pre-entry (academic year)

City of Liverpool Community College, Faculty of Adult & Continuing Education, Muirhead Centre, Muirhead Ave East, Liverpool L11 1ES;
0151 252 1515
Day release/Postgraduate one year

City University, Graduate Centre for Journalism, Northampton Square, London, EC1V 0HB; 0171 477 8000
Postgraduate one year/Degree

Cornwall College, Redruth, Cornwall TR15 3RD; 01209 712911
Pre-entry/Graduate fast track (20 weeks)

Darlington College of Technology, Cleveland Ave, Darlington, Co Durham DL3 7BB; 01325 503050
Pre-entry (academic and calendar year)/Degree

De Montfort University, The Gateway, Leicester LE1 9BH; 0116 255 1551
Postgraduate one year

Gloucester College of Art and Technology, Brunswick Campus, Brunswick Rd, Gloucester GL1 1HU; 01452 426549
Pre-entry (academic year)

Greenhill College, Lowlands Rd, Harrow, Middx HA1 3AQ; 0181 869 8600
Pre-entry (academic year)

Gwent Tertiary College, Pontypool & Usk Campus, Blaendare Rd, Pontypool, Gwent NP4 5YE; 01495 333100
Pre-entry academic year

Harlow College, College Square, The Hides, Harlow, Essex CM20 1LT; 01279 868000
Pre-entry/Graduate fast track (20 weeks)

Highbury College, Dovercourt Rd, Cosham, Portsmouth, Hampshire, PO6 2SA; 01705 283287
Block/Pre-entry (academic and calendar year)

Lambeth College, Vauxhall Centre, Belmore St, Wandsworth Rd, London SW8 2JY; 0171 501 5424
Postgraduate one year/pre-entry academic year

London College of Printing, School of Media, Back Hill, Clerkenwell, London EC1R 5EN; 0171 514 6500
Two-year HND

Napier University, Craighouse Campus, Craighouse Rd, Edinburgh EH10 5DT; 0131 444 2266
Degree

Sheffield College, Stradbroke Centre, Spinkhill Drive, Sheffield, South Yorkshire S13 8FD; 0114 260 2600
Postgraduate fast track (18 weeks)/Pre-entry (calendar and academic years)

South East Essex College of Art and Technology, Carnarvon Rd, Southend-on-Sea, Essex SS2 6LS; 01702 220400
Pre-entry (academic year)

Strathclyde University, 26 Richmond Street, Glasgow G1 1XH; 0141 553 4166
Postgraduate (one year)

Sutton Coldfield College, Lichfield Rd, Sutton Coldfield, West Midlands B74 2NW; 0121 355 5671
Pre-entry (academic year)

Trinity & All Saints College, Brownberry Lane, Horsforth, Leeds LS18 5HD; 0113 283 7100
Postgraduate (one year)

University of Central Lancashire, Centre for Journalism, Preston, Lancashire PR1 2HE; 01772 201201
Postgraduate (one year)/Pre-entry (academic year)/Degree

University of Sheffield, Journalism Studies, 171 Northumberland Road, Sheffield S10 2TZ; 0114 282 6730
Degree

University of Wales College of Cardiff , Journalism Studies Centre, 69
Park Place, Cardiff CF1 3AS; 01222 874786
Postgraduate (one year)/Degree

Warrington Collegiate Institute, Padgate Campus, Crab Lane,
Warrington WA2 0DB; 01925 814343
Day release

Wulfrun College, Paget Road, Wolverhampton WV6 0DU; 01902
317700
Day release

The following courses are recognized by the Periodicals Training
Council (PTC) and are relevant if you wish to pursue a career in
magazine journalism:

Journalism Training Centre, Mill Green Road, Mitcham, Surrey CR4
4HT; 0181 640 3696
14 week course, running three times a year

London College of Fashion, 20 St John Princes Street, London W1M
0DG; 0171 514 7400
Fashion degree with journalism and public relations options.

PMA Training, The Old Anchor, Church Street, Hemingford Grey,
Cambridgeshire PE18 9DF; 01480 300653
Postgraduate course in magazine journalism

University of Westminster, School of Communication, Harrow
Campus, Watford Road, Harrow HA1 3TP; 0171 911 5000
Postgraduate diploma in periodical journalism; part-time MA in
Journalism Studies; other postgraduate and short courses available

Newspaper in-company schemes

Some local newspaper companies have their own qualifications for
journalists, combining on-the-job assessment and exam-based study.
If you are accepted as a direct entry trainee on one of these papers,
you will undertake one of these courses. The following is a list of the

companies which provide this training. They may also have information on which papers within their group can offer jobs to direct entry trainees.

Trinity Editorial Training, Thomson House, Groat Market, Newcastle upon Tyne NE1 1ED; 0191 201 6043

Midland News Association, Rock House, Old Hill, Tettenhall, Wolverhampton, West Midlands WV6 8QB; 01902 313131

The Editorial Centre, Hanover House, Marine Court, St Leonards on Sea, East Sussex TN38 0DX; 01424 435991
(This used to be the Westminster Press Training Centre before a management buy-out)

NUJ accredited courses

The following courses are approved by the NUJ, which means that the prospectus has been studied by the union, and 'contains a sound practical and ethical element, with work placements and a fair record of students finding work'. An NUJ accredited course enables a student to become – free of charge – a temporary member of the union and obtain a press card.

Barnsley College, Honeywell Site, Honeywell Lane, Barnsley, South Yorkshire S75 IBP; 01226 730191
Combined studies degree with journalism pathway

Cleveland College of Art and Design, Green Lane, Linthorpe, Middlesbrough TS5 7RJ; 01642 821441
Two year HND in photography

CSV Media, Piccadilly Action, 2nd floor, Clayton House, 59 Piccadilly, Manchester M1 2AQ; 0161 228 3680
Postgraduate pre-entry course in newspapers

Edinburgh Media and Arts Training Trust, 4th floor, 28 Northbridge, Edinburgh EH1 1QG; 0131 225 9512
Open pre-entry course in newspapers

Hackney Community College, Keltan House, 89–115 Mare Street, London E8 4RS; 0181 985 8484
Access course in newspapers

Journalism Training Centre, Unit G, Mill Green Business Park, Mill Green, Mitcham, Surrey CR4 4HT; 0181 640 3696
Open pre-entry course in magazine journalism

Lambeth College, Department of Continuing Education, Vauxhall Section, Belmore Street, Wandsworth, London SW8 2JY; 0171 498 1234
Access and open pre-entry course in newspapers

Lewes Tertiary College, Media Studies Department, Mountfield Road, Lewes, East Sussex BN7 2XH; 01273 483188
Advanced GNVQ in media studies

London College of Fashion, 20 John Princes Street, London, W1M 0BJ; 0171 514 7400
Three-year degree in fashion journalism

North Cheshire College, Padgate Campus, Fernhand Lane, Warrington WA2 0DB; 01295 814343
Three-year BA in media studies

North Oxfordshire College, Broughton Road, Banbury OX16 9QA; 01295 252221
Access course in journalism

PMA Training, The Old Anchor, Church Street, Hemingford Gray, Cambridgeshire PE18 0DF; 01480 300653
Postgraduate pre-entry in magazine journalism

Southampton Institute of Higher Education, East Park Terrace, Southampton, SO9 4WW; 01703 229381
Three-year BA in journalism

Surrey Institute of Art and Design, Falkner Road, Farnham GU9 7DS;
01252 722441
Two-year HND or three-year degree course in print journalism

University of London, Birkbeck College Centre for Extra-Mural
Studies, 26 Russell Square, London WC1B 5DQ; 0171 631 6644
Certificate and diploma in media practice

University of Sunderland, School of Arts, Design and
Communication, Langham Tower, Ryhope Road, Sunderland SR2 7E;
0191 515 2157
Three-year BA in media studies

University of Westminster, Faculty of Law, Languages and
Communication, 18-22 Riding House Street, London W1P 7PD;
0171 911 5000
Three-year MA in journalism studies

University of Wolverhampton, School of Humanities and Social
Sciences, Dudley Campus, Castle View, Dudley DY1 3HR;
01902 321000
Three-year degree in media and communication studies

Wakefield College, Faculty of Performance Media and Arts, Margaret
Street, Wakefield, West Yorkshire WF1 2DH; 01924 370501
Three-year BA in media studies

Yale College, Wrexham FE Centre, Grove Park Road, Clwyd,
Wrexham LL12 7AA; 01978 311 794
Day-release course in newspapers

Further information on courses

You can obtain guides to training from the following organizations:

Newspaper Society, 74 Russell St, London WC1B 3DA;
0171 636 7014
It provides list of accredited courses. It also publishes the leaflet
'Training to be a Journalist', which has invaluable information.

British Film Institute, 21 Stephen St, London W1P 2LN;
0171 255 1444
It publishes *Media Courses UK*, which is updated annually and has a full listing of further education, undergraduate, and postgraduate media studies courses. Price £9.99.

National Council for the Training of Journalists (NCTJ), Latton Bush Centre, Southern Way, Harlow, Essex CM18 7BL; 01279 430009
The council, which is a charity, accredits courses at colleges and universities. It should be your first port of call for information on formal training.

Periodicals Training Council (PTC), Queens House, 28 Kingsway, London WC2B 6JR; 0171 404 4168
The PTC has been the training arm of the Periodical Publishers Associations since 1992. It was responsible for setting magazine NVQs and publishes an annual *Directory of Magazine Training*.

National Union of Journalists (NUJ), 314 Gray's Inn Road, London WC1X 8DP; 0171 278 7916
Publishes a booklet: *Careers in Journalism*.

Training with the nationals

There are limited places available on national newspapers, mostly for graduate trainees. As a rule, national newspapers tend to recruit from the regions, allowing them to pick journalists who are already fully trained and experienced. The following, though, do have training schemes:

The Express offers up to five places a year to graduates who wish to become journalists. Trainees work for two years at *The Express*, with three-month placements in different departments, so that they can gain a range of experience. The positions are now not advertised in the press and around 90 people sent in applications for places in 1997. Competition, however, is fierce. While *The Express* does not guarantee the trainee a position at the end of the contracted period, some are offered jobs at the end of either their first or second year. The starting salary is £13,260 rising to £13,770 in the second year.

For further information write to the Group Managing Editor at the address below.

The Express, Ludgate House, 254 Blackfriars Road, London SE1 9UX

The Telegraph group has recently launched a one-year training scheme for six young journalists. Students who have completed a postgraduate course in journalism will be given priority. You must also have some examples of published material. Write to the Head of Editorial Training.

The Daily Telegraph, 1 Canada Square, Canary Wharf, London E14 5DT

The Scott Trust, owners of *The Guardian*, sponsor bursary places on postgraduate diploma courses. Four places are offered at the City University and two places at the Department of Journalism, University of Central Lancashire in Preston. Each bursary will cover the cost of course fees and provide £4,000 towards living expenses, plus work experience placements on the group's local and regional newspapers. For information, write to the Scott Trust Bursary at either:

Department of Journalism, City University, Northampton Square, London EC1V 0HB
or Department of Journalism, University of Central Lancashire, Preston PR1 2HE

If you are from an African, Asian or Caribbean background, *The Sunday Times* offers a fellowship to those who have already started on a journalistic career or graduates who have left university with experience of student newspapers. Formal training and practical experience alongside staff journalists will be given. Write to the Editor, John Witherow.

The Sunday Times, 1 Pennington Street, London E1 9XW

Glossary

All-in: a pack of journalists descend on someone to ask them questions.

Angle: an aspect of a story about which the journalist writes.

Bi-medial: the ability of a journalist to be able to work in two media, ie radio and television, or radio and newspapers.

Breakout quote: an eye-catching quote from the copy that appears in a separate box on the newspaper page.

Broadsheet: the largest format newspaper. Also a term that refers to a style of journalism regarded as more serious and analytical. Opposite of **Tabloid** (see below).

By-line: the writer's name, sometimes accompanied by a picture.

Caption: a description of a picture.

Circulation: the number of papers sold.

Colour supplement: old-fashioned term to describe colour magazines in newspapers.

Column: news and features copy is flowed into newspaper columns; it is the short form for a personal column written by a journalist.

Commission: a request from a features editor or commissioning editor to write a story for payment.

Conference: held several times a day (morning and evening) by the editor to decide what will go into the newspaper. Sometimes impromptu when news demands it.

Contacts: people a reporter speaks with in order to find about stories.

Copy: the text written by a journalist.

Copy approval: where a celebrity or similar is allowed to see and approve the copy before it goes into print.

Correspondent: a term to describe a certain type of journalist, such as a crime correspondent.

Cross reference: a small heading at the end of a story to point the reader to a connected or relevant story on another page. It can also say on which page the story continues.

Cuttings job: a type of profile where the journalist writes from a series of cuttings from other newspapers or publications.

Doorstop: type of interview in which you ask someone questions outside their home or work.

Death knock: calling on the relative of a victim to interview them.

Dumbing down: the process by which low brow or less challenging items are favoured editorially over more cerebral ones.

Fact box: a box detailing some relevant pieces of information to the main story on the page.

Feature: a story that brings to light a distinctive part or aspect of an issue, person or event.

Freelance: a journalist who works independently rather than with one publication. Also known as a **Stringer**.

Handouts: press releases sent to journalists.

Hack: another word for a journalist or reporter.

Headline: bold copy at the head of the story, which is used to draw the readers' attention.

Hook: generally included in the intro to a feature, the hook can be a topical reference around which a story is based. Also known as the **Peg**.

Intro: the first sentence of a story which, in news, outlines the most important facts. Also known as the **Lead** or **Nose**.

Leader: a newspaper's editorial.

Libel: where a journalist damages someone's reputation with an untruth.

National: a national newspaper or magazine.

News: a story about someone or something that is new, interesting and may affect our lives.

News facts: who, what, where, when, why, how. The six facts that should be included in a news story.

NIBs: Literally, news in brief.

NUJ: National Union of Journalists.

Obituary: profile of someone's life after they have died.

Off the record: information gathered by the journalist which cannot be directly quoted in a story. Opposite of **On the record**.

Paparazzi: literally, a horde of photographers who pursue celebrities for photographs.

Pay-off: the last line of a feature which makes some sort of conclusion.

PCC: Press Complaints Commission, which issues a code of practice for journalists.

Photojournalism: the use of pictures to tell a news or feature story.

Piece: literally, a piece of copy or story.

Press: a term that describes newspapers as a whole, or physically what newspapers are printed with.

Profile: a feature story about someone's life, based on an interview or cuttings.

Puff: a type of press release or story that is designed to give maximum publicity.

Quote: direct speech.

Readership: the number of people reading the newspaper, which is always more than the actual circulation because households generally have more than person.

Reporter: a journalist who gathers the news.

Running story: one that has been reported before and is continuing in some way.

Scheme: the sketch or design of a page that shows where each story will appear when it is printed.

Shoot: an organized session at which a photographer takes pictures.

Side-bar: a panel running down the outside of the newspaper with a story linked to the main item on the page.

Snapper: photographer, also known as a **Monkey**.

Sources: where the story has come from, either a person or organization. A story can have several different sources.

Spike: where a story goes when it has been rejected.

Standfirst: a short introductory sentence which stands apart from the main story. Also known as the **Sell**.

Story: the basic element in journalism.

Strapline: a line of copy that appears across the top of the page as a secondary headline. Sometimes just called the **Strap**.

Structure: how a story fits together and which elements are used.

Tabloid: A3 sized printed page. A style of journalism that implies a more superficial and less in-depth coverage of the news.

Tone: the feel of a story – serious, humorous, etc.

Typeface: the style of lettering, such as Times or Courier. Also known as **Font**.

Vox pop: a straw poll of members of the public about a particular issue.

Answers

Chapter 3

Exercise 1

Consumers' Association; National Consumers Council; water authority (is there a change in the water?); retail outlets (have there been
other complaints?); kettle manufacturers; electricity companies;
university academic on electrical engineering; readers who have
similar kettle and toaster problems.

Exercise 2

1. It has been alleged that you took a bribe before last year's semi-
   final. Is this true?
2. How do you account for the story?
3. What is your relationship with *The Daily Mirror*?
4. How do you explain the semi final loss?
5. Are you going to resign as manager?

Exercise 3

1. Will you be watching Comic Relief tonight? YES/SOME OF
   IT/NO
2. Will you be donating any money? YES/NO/DON'T KNOW
3. Do you think telethons should try to make you feel guilty?
   YES/NO
4. When was the last Comic Relief Day? MARCH 1996/MARCH
   1997/DON'T KNOW
5. Do you give to charity? YES/NO/OCCASIONALLY
6. How would you fund charities, if it all?

Chapter 4

Exercise 1

1. *Who*: Archbishop of York, John Habgood.
    What: Called for tax cuts for married people
    When: Today
2   *Who*: woman police officer.
    What: raped by a male colleague after New Year party.
    When: court heard yesterday (in this instance it is when it was reported in the court, not when the incident actually happened).
3. *Who*: wealthy Tory activist.
    What: shot dead by his son.
    When: an inquest was told yesterday (not when the actual death occurred).
4. *Who*: Diane Blood.
    What: cleared hurdle to use dead husband's sperm.
    When: last night.
5. *Who*: Russian Defence Ministry.
    What: reached deal with Chechen forces.
    When: last night.

Exercise 2

A London restaurant may have to close after its owner and staff shared this week's £20m jackpot in the National Lottery.

Regular customers at a London restaurant are worried that their favourite eating place may close after its owner and staff shared this week's £20m jackpot.

Exercise 3

Jill and Tony Pascoe and their son Daniel were asleep in the upstairs bedrooms of the house in Waley Street when fire broke out downstairs after a gas explosion.

Mr Walsh, 30, said 'It was a nightmare. The whole thing just went bang. It was an enormous explosion.'

Fire officer David Pascoe, who led the rescue, said 'I managed to get the parents out first, Jill and Tony, but couldn't find their young baby Daniel anywhere.

'I looked everywhere. Finally I found him under a wardrobe in the bedroom. The blast had been so strong that he had been blown under there. It was just luck that I found him.'

Mr Walsh said he hoped fire officer Pascoe would be commended. 'We all owe our lives to fire officer Pascoe who got us out. I really didn't think he was going to find Daniel. He deserves a medal. It was fantastic.'

Fire chief William Green said: 'We think it was a gas blast. It's a miracle that anyone got out alive. We will be considering a medal for Pascoe.'

Chapter 5

Exercise 1

1. Kirsty Young, Outside Edge personal column.
2. Ysenda Maxtone Graham, personal column.
3. News feature on spate of Titanic films.
4. William Hickey, gossip column.
5. Film review of Portrait of a Lady.

Exercise 2

1. Looks like the word is out – save money.
2. Charlie, just like his audiences, will no doubt be driven up the wall.
3. Perhaps Mr Beard Trimmer does lessons in his spare time.

Exercise 3

1. On a quiet May morning in Soho, Charlie Parsons of Planet 24 fame is walking towards me. He strides out purposefully, but where is the chauffeur?
2. The Big Breakfast, Britain's outrageously good morning television knockabout, is set to bounce back in the ratings war to renew the fortunes of Planet 24 – a chauffeurless Charlie Parsons must-wish.
3. Can you name one of Britain's most successful television companies whose creative top dog is without a chauffeur?
4. 'Charlie's chauffeur, Kit, is leaving today,' said the man with the beard trimmer.

(There is no right or wrong way to write an intro. These are suggested intros.)

Chapter 6

Exercise 1

1. Are you still having fun?
2. What does it feel like after 50 years?
3. Is this the best line-up?
4. How relevant is your music?
5. Why are you still doing it?
6. What are you working on?
7. What is your 'working day' now?
8. What do you think of modern music?
9. Were you and the Beatles a one-off?
10. Will you ever retire?

Further reading

Brendan Hennessy and FW Hodgson (1995) *Journalism Workbook: A Manual of Tasks, Projects and Resources*, Focal Press

Richard Keeble (1994) *The Newspapers Handbook*, Routledge, London

Joan Clayton (1992) *Journalism for Beginners, How to Get Into Print and Get Paid For It*, Piatkus, London

Index

advertising   63
all-ins   36
angle   11, 46, 92
art editor   116

background   42
    features   85
backgrounders   66
bi-medial   1
Booth, Tony   104
Boulevard magazine   83, 91
breaking news   59
Bridgewater Three case   44
British Film Institute   129
broadsheet   12
bucket question   35

cannabis   35
captions   110
celebrities   80
Chancellor of the Exchequer   31
checking   55, 108
chief sub-editor   116
Clinton, President   9
Code of Practice   12
colour   29, 85, 90
conference   3
confidence   5
contacts   16
Conservative Party   4

copy approval   85, 91
copyboy   115
copyright   86
cuttings job   86

death knocks   37
dedication   2
determination   2
Diana, Princess of Wales   9
direct entry   118
doorstops   36
drama   10

editor   117
embarrassing questions   89
ethics   3

face-to-face interviews   82, 87
features
    general   61
    definition   63
    types   65
    service   68
    structure   72
    intros   75
features editor   16

Geldof, Bob   73
glossary   131
grammar   109
handouts   22

Hattersley, Roy   77, 97
headlines   110
heavies   12
Hello   80
Hickey, William   73
Hitchen Brian   21
home secretary   9
hook   11, 93
humour   3
human intrest   8

imagination   3
information journalism   1
Ingham, Sir Bernard   82
inquisitiveness   2
intelligence   2
interviewing   24
    face to face   88
intro   40, 47
    features   75
    question   78
    quote   78

Labour   4
lead   75
leader articles   98
Leibowitz, Annie   113
libel   96

Major, John   7
making calls   18
managing editor   116
media studies courses   120
middleweight celebrities   80
Modern Apprenticeship   118,
    119
Monkhouse, Bob   102
multi-medial   1
National Council for the Training

of Journalists   120, 122,
    129
National Union of Journalists   3,
    126
National Vocational Qualification
    15, 119,
news
    what is   8
news editor   116
news maker   9
newspaper in-company schemes
    125
Newspaper Society   128
news peg   76
news story   4
    structure   39, 53
newsworthy   9
night editor   116
NUJ accredited courses   126

off the record   25
on the record   24
op ed   24
opinion pieces   67

paparazzi   113
pay-off   65, 74
personal columns   68, 102
Periodical Training Council
    129
photojournalism   111
picture editor   116
pigeon racers   9
Pitt, Brad   83
possibles   5
pre-entry   120
Press Complaints Commission
    (PCC)   4, 12, 18, 113
press conferences   27

proactive   14
production journalism   107
profiles
    general   67, 80
    types   82
    structure   83
public relations (PRs)   29, 32,
    91
puff   91
pyramid concept   34
    inverted   93

qualities   4
quotes   93

reporter   115
reporting   14
rewriting   109
resourcefulness   3
researcher   115
reviews   69, 94
Rolling Stones   94
Royal Family   4, 9
rubber chicken circuit   31
running stories   59

Salaries   122, 129
shorthand   120
Simpson, OJ   17
snappers   5, 88
speeches   31

Sport, The   90
standfirst   123
Star, Daily   71
Starr, Freddie   12
Stephens, Toby   78
straw poll   34
style   69
sub-editor   107, 115
Sun, The   19

tabloid   11
teaser intro   77
Teletubby   22
Telegraph, Daily   130
Thatcher, Lady   82
Times, Sunday   84, 130
tone   70, 85
training   114, 118
truth   12
Training and Enterprise Councils
    119
typical journalist   4
vox pop   34

Waugh, Evelyn   8
Who What Where When Why
    and How...?   21, 48, 89
Woodard, Louise   17

Young, Kirsty   64